Aylesbury Grammar School
1598 – 1998
A Commemorative Volume

W. R. MEAD

SIR HENRY LEE

Aylesbury
Grammar School
1598 – 1998

a Commemorative
Volume
by W. R. MEAD

With a Foreword

by The Right Honourable

LORD ROTHSCHILD

THE PETERHOUSE PRESS

Published in Great Britain
for the School
by the Peterhouse Press,
Brill, Aylesbury, England

Copyright © W. R. Mead

ISBN 0 946312 06 0

CONTENTS

List of Illustrations   vii
Foreword The Rt. Hon. Lord Rothschild   ix
Preface   xi
Tabula Gratulatoria   xiii

Part One – The Old School

Sir Henry Lee and the Donations   1
Phillips' Gift   6
Building the Old School   12
Ordering the Free School   14
'Deviations from the Regulations'   22
A Greenfield Site   41
Building the New School   47
The Legacy of the Old School   50

Part Two – The Mixed School

'The Beginning of the New'   53
The War Years and After   61
A Meeting of History and Memory   69
A Decade of Consolidation   70
'Schooling in an Emergency'   79
Post-War Changes   85
The Passing of the Mixed School   96

Part Three – The New School

A New Beginning   107
A Time of Fulfilment   114
Floreat Aylesburia   134

APPENDICES

A – The Endowment at Broughton   141

B – 'A Scheme for the Management of the Aylesbury
        Free and Endowed Schools' 15 July, 1862   151

C – Boys at the School, 1997-98   157

D – School Governors, 1997-98   167

E – A Note on the Staff at the School 1678-1900   169

F – Staff at the School, 1997-98   171

G – A Note on Sources   175

Bibliography   177

LIST OF ILLUSTRATIONS

Page

ii Frontispiece. Portrait of Sir Henry Lee attributed to Marcus Gheeraerts the younger

3 Portrait of Sir Henry Lee by Antonio Mor (or Moro)

7 Photograph of the portrait of Henry Phillips that was destroyed in the fire, 1953

8 Mural monuments in St. Mary's Church, Aylesbury to Henry Phillips and Matthew Dagnall

16 Account for the payment of builders of the school for the week ending June 6, 1719

19 A mid-nineteenth century sketch of the old school

23 Robert Gibbs (1816-93)

25 The plan of the school in 1852

28 A page from the Register of Leavers' details, 1844

30 A page from the Admissions Register, 1900

35 A page from the Prize Book, 1860-1924

38 The site of the old school in Church Street

42 The site of the new school in Walton Road

43 A part of the memorandum of agreement for the transfer of the Walton Street land

45 Boys in the garden of the old school, 1904

51 Thomas Osborne, M.A. Oxon, Headmaster 1907-27

56 Staff and pupils, 1907-08

64 The school room from the 1720s as it was in the 1920s

66 The football team, 1924-25

67 Improvements being made to the playing field

72   The opening of the pavilion
74   The first page of the school song
76   Dress regulations in the inter-war years
80   Cricket Team 1930s
83   The teaching staff in the late 1940s,
        Headmaster G.P. Furneaux, M.A. Oxon
91   C.A.G. Pope's orchestra about 1952
97   L.W. Tidmarsh, M.A. Oxon, Headmaster, 1951-67
99   The physics laboratory after the fire in 1953
101 Hurdling in 1952
102 The girls' tennis team c.1955
103 The start of the cross-country run c.1958
106 Visit to Paris 1938
108 *A Midsummer Night's Dream,* 1960
111 Construction of the tower block
113 The squash team, 1976
115 The rugby seven, 1977
117 K.D. Smith, M.A. Cantab. Headmaster 1967-69
        and the Lord Mayor of London
121 *The Observer* mace
122 The cricket team in Trinidad and Tobago
125 Doctor's Orders
127 Ian Roe, B.A., Headmaster 1992–
129 The Jazz Band
131 The computer room in action
133 Plan of the expansion of the school premises
142 The Enclosure Award for part of the Broughton
        property, July 15, 1780
144 A survey of the estate at Broughton c.1830
145 Memorandum of agreement for conveyance of
        land to Aylesbury Railway Company, 1838
148 Land in possession of the Foundation
        Governors at Broughton
156 The Head Boys and Heads of the six houses,
        1997-98
172 The school staff, 1997-98

FOREWORD

by The Right Honourable
LORD ROTHSCHILD

It gives me immense pleasure to congratulate Aylesbury Grammar School on its four hundredth birthday. The school can well and truly claim to be part of the heritage of Buckinghamshire – indeed, part of our national heritage. It is a happy coincidence that the celebrations are being held at a time when the achievements of the school may have never been more notable.

The occasion is a particularly happy one for me too, for it restores the links that my family has had with the school over many years. At the turn of the century, the Foundation Trustees were looking for a site for the new Mixed School and they were able to persuade my great grand-father, Lord Rothschild of Tring, to let go two fields in Walton Road. Ninety years ago, when the new school building was completed, Lord Rothschild opened the door with a silver key and made the principal speech. As a good environmentalist he even provided trees and shrubs for the front garden. Only seven years later, the school was taken over by the War Office as a military hospital. After the armistice, it appears that it was my cousin, Lionel de Rothschild, Member of Parliament for the constituency, who was able to use his influence to speed the return of the building to the school.

I can even claim an indirect link with one of your two founders, Sir Henry Lee and Henry Phillips. The land surrounding Eythrope Estate, where I now live, must have had a common boundary with the ances-tral estate of Sir Henry. Doubtless some of his legendary flock of three thousand sheep strayed from time to time across the open fields from Quarrendon.

It is remarkable to reflect upon the progress of the school – from the 20 boys for whom Sir Henry's donation provided the initial schooling (with the vicar of Aylesbury their solitary master), through the 120 boys from Aylesbury and Walton and their three teachers in the new school Henry Phillips made possible, to the 1,100 boys and seventy staff of today. The Vale of Aylesbury is indeed fortunate to have such a remarkable school. I wish it all success during its anniversary year and continued good fortune in the new millennium.

Rothschild

PREFACE

This book belongs to the retrospective part of the commemoration of four hundred years of Aylesbury Grammar School. The story falls into three parts. The record of the old school with its limited resources is well settled into history. The mixed school lies at the meeting ground of memory and history and can be dealt with in the round. The burgeoning story of the present school can only be selective in its content. While it aims to include the most important trends in the school's development, it must necessarily limit reference to the infinity of day-to-day activities and to the many personalities who have contributed to them.

Publication is taking place at the beginning of a year of celebration, the foundations for which have been well and truly laid by the splendid response to the anniversary appeal. The William Harding trustees led the way and set the appeal in motion with a most generous contribution. They have been followed by British Aerospace, Research Machines PLC, S-Com Computer Systems Ltd., Con. Dev. Europe Ltd., The Frost Group PLC, Compusys Ltd. and the National Westminster Bank PLC. Some four hundred parents (past as well as present), former pupils, staff, governors and local well-wishers have made individual covenanted donations. The results will be clearly seen in the fulfilment of a number of long-awaited projects.

The preparation and publication of the text has been undertaken by a committee consisting of Polly Wilkinson, Ashley Robson, Peter Medcalf and the author under the chairmanship of Ian Roe who has been a source of unfailing help and encouragement. Polly Wilkinson undertook an initial sifting of much of the material from the post-war period. Her enthusiasm and help were invaluable at a difficult stage in the preparation of the text. K.D. Smith contributed significantly to the section covering the period of his headship. The Rev. Arthur Taylor and Hugh Hanley have commented most helpfully on matters both of detail and the broader historical setting. Susan Roe has been an indispensable proof reader. A very considerable debt is owed to Vanessa Kennedy for her patience in typing – and retyping – the manuscript.

The committee is grateful to present and former members of the school as well as to many others who have sent reminiscences or have provided specialised help. It is impossible to include all of them, but mention must be made of Professor Ian Beckett, Roger Bettridge, Linda Bomken, Daphne Eggar, Barbara Fell (née Gunstone), Margaret Furneaux, Sarah Gray (County Museum), Chris Harper (Photographer), Frederick Hinxman, Julian Hunt (County Reference Library), A.W. Hurst, R. Lloyd-Jones, Dennis Lack, Margaret Lowe, Geraldine Maison, Muriel Moore (née Waters), John Reed, Professor Michael Reed, Jasmine Reeks, James Robbins, Mary Staff (née Mays), Mark Tapping, Joy Waters, Robert Wilson and Simon Winman. A special file of letters received during the preparation of the book has been placed in the school archive.

It will be noted that there is inconsistency in the style of address of the many people mentioned in the text. Prior to the time of the New School, Mr., Mrs. and Miss were usually employed. Subsequently, Christian and surnames are generally used unless there is a formal title.

Finally, this book would not have been possible without the highly professional assistance of the Publishers Peter Medcalf and his son Paul. The school owes them a debt of gratitude for all that they have done towards producing a worthy commemorative volume.

September 14, 1997

(September 14 was Henry Phillips' birthday, on which date the original trustees were enjoined to meet annually)

Note. Certain references have been left in the text for the benefit of anyone wishing to refer to the original documents in the Buckinghamshire Record Office e.g. B.R.O./CH3/L2/14.

TABULA GRATULATORIA

Mr & Mrs M Ageli
Nicholas J Ainger
Andrew Albrighton
Philip Albrighton
E W J Alder
Geoffrey Aldridge
Hilary Aldridge (née Ratcliffe)
Sam Alexander
Jill Allen
Freda Anderson (née Waters)
Douglas Andrew
Mr A D & Mrs M M Andrews
Mr & Mrs Douglas Andrews
Anthony A W Arnold
Mr & Mrs R Arrowsmith
Mr & Mrs S C Ash
Hazel (née Goodyer) & Brian
   Attwood
Mr & Mrs F Auld
David Aylett & Patricia Aylett (née
   McHale)
Veronica Aylward
Thomas Ayres
Dr Roland Bailey
Mr & Mrs A J Baker
Mr R & Mrs G Baker
Mr & Mrs S Baker
Timothy Baker
Mr A Balch
Mr & Mrs M M Banfield
Damian Banks
Nathan Banks
Simeon Banks
Mr & Mrs R J Bansback
Martin D Barlow
Jean Barnard (née Irvine)
Daniel Barrett
Mrs M A Barrett

Tony Barrett
Norman & Patsy Bartlett
Phyllis Bartlett
Freda M Barton
Jolyon James John Bates
E H & Mrs P M Beales
Simon P Beattie
Professor Ian F W Beckett
M E A Beckowicz
Mr & Mrs Belam
Gottfried & Jean Belger
James Bellin
Larry & Alison Benjamin
Mr Peter Bianca & Mrs Zsuzsanna
   Bianca
Helen M Biggs
Mr & Mrs John W Biggs
Angela Billingham (née Case), M.E.P.;
   J.P.
Ron Blaxter
James E Bomken
Simon N Bomken
Dr K R Bond
John Bonham
Simon G Boots
David M F Botell
Patrick J F Botell
Jon Bottomley
Nicholas Bottomley
Andrew Bourbon
James D S Bowe
William T S Bowe
Mr & Mrs A W Bowes
Mr & Mrs Paul A Bown & Family
Dr & Ms Boyd-Kirkup
Mrs June Bradshaw
Mrs N Brewer
Mr & Mrs D Brooker

Mrs B A Brown
Mr & Mrs B C Brown
D Brown
David & Karen Brown
E P Brown
Ben J Brownlee
Peter & Pat Brunt
Bucks County Council
Mrs Margaret Budd
Mr R G Budd
Mary Bulloch
Mrs D Burnett
Mrs Marilyn Burrows
Richard Bursby
John, Shirley, Kieran & Rebecca Bush
Linda & Colin Butler
David & Rachel Butler
J R & D J Cadwallader
David Callus, ISO FRICS
Mr & Mrs D P Cann
Mr Sean D Cannon
R M Carey
P Carpenter
Daniel J Carr
Luke Carr
Ken & Ann Carr-Barnsley
R Donovan Carter
Jonathan Martin Caswell
Mr & Mrs T K Chandler
Oliver Chantler
Mr J & Mrs A Chapman
Mrs G N Hillsdon/Michael Chilton
Mr & Mrs Steven Choy
Mr & Mrs Arthur J Christian
Mr & Mrs E Chu
Michael Clibbon
Sue Clibbon
Mr Ted Cockle
Mr & Mrs J Cogger
Mrs E G Cole
Cecily A Collingridge
Mr & Mrs J D Collins

John H Collins
David John Colvin, BSc, CEng,
    MIMechE
Andrew Cooke
Roger & Denise Lesley Cooper
Clive O Cooper
Michael & Maureen Cooper
Mr & Mrs Richard Cooper
D C Cooper
N L Copcutt
Revd Ivor Cornish
Ian Cornish
Sam Cottman
Mr & Mrs T J Cotton
Fraser Neil Coutts
Mr James H Cox & Mrs Irene Cox
    (née Phipps)
Max Craft
Mrs Joan Crichlow (née Allin)
Dennis James Cripps
Mr & Mrs P J B Croker
Brian Crook
Andrew M Cross
David G Cross
Jan & Christopher Cross
Mrs S J Crowle
Edward John Curtis
Mr & Mrs R Curtis
Richard & Ann Curtis
Colin Cutler
David & Sylvia Cutler
Ian Cutler
Neil Cutler
The Dablin Family
Dr & Mrs K W Daisley
Mr & Mrs E A Davenport
Roy Davenport
Diane Davies
Hamilton Davies
Bruce Davis
Christopher Davis
Peter Davis

Marion Dawson
Brian, Gill, Andrew & Steven Dean
P J & J M Deay
Martin & Susan Deli for Gareth Deli
Martyn R Dennis
Mrs J A Dennis (née Lloyd)
Mrs Lynda M Dix, BSc; Mr Stephen
    Dix, BSc
Phyllis Dix (Mrs)
Matt Dodds
Stephen & Susan Donohoe
Don Dormer
Mr & Mrs M Draper
Graham John Dubberley
Alexis Dubus
Mrs M C Duffy
Aidan Eardley
Alexander Eardley
Barbara Eastop (née Harris)
Daphne Ridgway Edgar
Alan D Edwards
Matthew & Laura Edwards
Brian & Hafswa Ellis
John N Elsden
Mrs G Ennis
Edward Evans
Justin, Jason, Peter & David Evans
Muriel Lily Joyce Evans
Robert R Evans
Betty Evett (née Winter)
Margaret Elizabeth Evett (née Carter)
Dr Ann Fahy (née Colvin)
John Faulkner
Terry & Nicola Faulkner
Mr & Mrs J Fazakerley
Barbara Fell (née Gunstone)
Mr & Mrs Casimer J Fernandez
J W & M A Ferris
Christine Fleet
The Fox Family
Ronald A Francis
Sylvia Francis (née Stedeford)

James R M Franklin
Mr & Mrs M A Fuchter
F K Furley (Mrs)
Noel & Pat Furley
Margaret Furneaux
Sir Peter Gadsden
Neville A R Gelling
K T & J A Gibbons
Dr & Mrs M J Gibby
Martin & Sandra Giddings
Peter & Julia Giles
The Gill Family
Tim Glenton
Mrs T Glover
Richard N Gommo
Lou Rita Goodhope
Matthew & Stephen Goodright
Rhys & Huw Goodwin
Don Gordon; Alison Gordon
Bill & Marjorie Grace
John Grace
S G Grace
Mr & Mrs I H T Graham
Dr R J & Mrs Grayson
Anthony Green
Daniel Green
P E Green
Mark Greenfield
Mr & Mrs W A Gregory
John Peter Groves
Richard & Mary Gurney
David & Valerie Hall
The Hall Family
Mr & Mrs C J Hallsworth
Mrs Hilda M Halsey (née Biggerstaff)
Mrs Betty Hampton
Brian & Linda Hancock
Mr & Mrs I R Hancock
Tim Hancock
Mrs Ann E Handshaw
John Harcourt
K B & E Hardern

Mr & Mrs C F D Hart
Mr & Mrs R M Hartley
Brian & Carol Haselgrove
Mr & Mrs N Hastings
Mrs Valerie A Havard (née Pearson)
P M Hayes
John Roland Haynes
H A J Helliwell
Dennis A Higgins
James Higginson
David Philip Hillier
Mr & Mrs R E Hills
Mrs A C Hillsdon
Betty M Hiscock (née Payne)
Mr & Mrs R M Hocking
Paul, Linda, Matthew, Lee & Sophie
    Hodges
Simon Hodges
D M & W Hodgkinson
Mrs Margaret Hoffmann (née Ballad)
John R Holmes
Mr S J & Mrs V A Holmes
Professor V Holopainen
Mrs J Holton
Gwyneth & Ian Horn and Family
Molly Houghton (née Ettrick)
M F & D A Houldsworth
Mrs Kathy Howard
Paul Hrycyszyn
Mr A T & Mrs A Hulse
Mr & Mrs S Hunter
A W Hurst
Timothy Iredale
Rev Fred Ireland
Mr & Mrs Stephen James
Mr & Mrs R W Jeffery
Brenda Jennings
Paul Jennings
Mrs Phyllis Jenns
Ben John
Tony Johns
Christine & Len Jones

Derek W Jones
Linda & Graham Jones
Dr & Mrs M H Jones
Sue & Ken Jones
Mr Ted Jones
Susan & Martin Judd
Professor Eino Jutikkala
D W Keep
Richard & Denise Kemp
Moira & Richard Kendall
David & Vanessa Kennedy, James &
    Andrew Tovey
James Kent, BEng RAF
John R Kent
Adam John Killip
Benjamin T J King
Edwin A King
Edward A King
Stuart King
Roger & Sue Kirk
Dr & Mrs James K Kirkwood
Alan Kittles
David M Krause
Sylvia N Lacey (née Bird)
Dennis C Lack
Sylvia E Ladyman
Mr & Mrs F Laferton
Rosemary Lake
Keith Robert Lamdin
James Lane
Thomas Lane
Janet Langdon
P J Larkham
Mr & Mrs R W Lawson
Margaret L Leeks (née White)
Richard Leggett
Graham R Lewis
Dr & Mrs D Lewton
R J M Lloyd-Jones
D & Mrs K Loader
The Very Revd Dr H Lockley
Dr S & Mrs J Logsdail

Miss Margaret Lowe
Adrian Lowndes-Knight
Alec Lowndes-Knight
Mr & Mrs S J Lyon
Nigel & Caroline Lyons
Thomas I W MacMillan
Mrs Aino Maki
Robin & Sue Malduca
Joan Malpass (née Davies)
Mr G W Mann
Mr David John Marsh
James E Marsh
Mr & Mrs P C Marsh
Mrs Patricia J L Marsh (née Moran)
Mr Stephen Marsh
Mr & Mrs D Marshall
Stuart Marshall
Deborah J Marston
Kevin I M Marston
Mr K H & Mrs B H Martin
Joan Matthewson (née Bunce)
Dr & Mrs R W Mayes
Andrew W Mays
Mary Mays
Mr Simon J McBride
Drs Eric & Ruth McCairns
Dr R A McKenzie
V McLean
Mr & Mrs W McMeekin
Mr J H Mead
Mr C R Mead
Christopher J Melville
Mr & Mrs D C Merriman
Ian & Louise Metherell
A & J Middleton
Suzanne Millard
Andrew S Miller
Mr E W J & Mrs P Miller
Rowland Minall
Mrs G M M Miscampbell
Edward J M Mitchell
Mrs L Mitchell

Ian Money
Edward Philip Moody
Graham Andrew Moody
Muriel Moore (née Waters)
Mr & Mrs R P Moore
Leila Mary Morgan (née Badger)
Thomas Allan Morgan
Philip J Morris
Mr & Mrs Robert J Murphy
Heather Murray
Richard Muschamp
Mr & Mrs A J Mylles
Mr & Mrs Daniel Nash
Loveday Nelson (née Furneaux)
Mr & Mrs M New
Ruby Elizabeth New
Catherine Newson
Beryl Newton
Drs D & A Nicholas
J D & D M Nicholson
Pauline & Tony Noble
Mr & Mrs C Nodder
Philip & Vivien Nuckley
Cornelius G O'Donovan
Old Aylesburians' Association
Colin Oliver
Rosemary O'Lone
David Orchard
James Osborne, 1988 - 1993
Mrs D A Ottridge (née Patricia
    Stratford)
Wing Commander S D Ottridge
Mr T C Ottridge
Jeremy M Owen
Colin F Page
Derek & Christine Palmer
Jeanette Palmer (née Colley)
Ben & Tom Pammenter
Martin & Diana Parker
Mr & Mrs Nicholas John Parsons
Mr & Mrs M Partner
Mrs Patricia M Pascoe-Ellis

Andrew Paterson
Mr & Mrs A Paterson
Ian Paterson
J M A Paterson
Mr & Mrs R I Paterson
H E L Patten
Iain & Pauline Patterson
Selina Vinayaga-Pavan
Brian H Paxton
Kevin Paxton
Charles & Dorothy Pearce
Mr & Mrs G S Pearce
Mike Pearce
R G Pearce & Mrs A A Pearce
R & W M Pearman
Kenneth W Pearson
David & John Pennicott
Arthur M Perry
Vera Pether (née Maskelyne)
Diane, Chris & Ben Pickard
Ahrum Pilendiram
Dr & Mrs D N Pim
N Geoffrey J Pipe
Mr & Mrs Donald Pirkis
Ivor C Plater
Andrew Poole
Fred Pooley, CBE
Dr G A Porthouse
Patrick, Rosemary & Jeremy Powell
Richard Preece
Robert Prestidge
Simon Pridgeon
John & Pauline Prior
Mr & Mrs Roy Pritchard
Mr J A Prodger
Mr Dennis Putman
Mr & Mrs C H Radley
Mr & Mrs G H Radley
Mr & Mrs S A Rae
Dr & Mrs D J Rainford
Donald R N Rand
Kathleen A Raven, D.B.E., O.St.J.,

F.R.C.N (Foundation Governor)
Colin Ravenhill
Mr & Mrs T Ray
Mr & Mrs J Read
Albin John Reed
Michael Reed
Mr & Mrs S D Reid-Perkin
Robert & June Renshaw
Mr P J & Mrs S J Reynier
Clive Rhodes
Neil Rickus
Andrew B Ridgway
Mr Glen Ridgway
N R H Ridgway
Andrew Rixon
B J Roberts
Mary Roberts (née Mullin)
James W Robins
Andrew Robinson
V J Robinson
Ian & Sue Roe
Nigel P J Roe
Paul John Rogers
Martin & Julia Roper
Mr & Mrs T F Ross
Alexander W Rothwell
Mrs L Rowett
William D L Rumsey
Pat & Allan Ruxton
Connie Ryall
Jon Anders Ryste
Mr M Sage
Nicholas Salter
Donald James Sanford
Paul Savage
Brian & Marianne Selby
R J & L K Senior
A M & E M Sessa
Mr & Mrs John Seward
James Shaw
Mr T J & Mrs P K Shepherd
Claude M A Shields

Mark Shilton
Martin & Wendy Shrubsole
Gavinash C Sirisena
Tim Skedge
Andrew J Small
Mrs Rachel Smart
Christopher Smith
Colin F W Smith
Gloria Smith (née Jarvis)
K D Smith
Mr & Mrs L Smith
Robert L Smith
Mr Edward Smithson
Mr & Mrs M J Snell
Jason C Soley
Phyllis Solloway
Mr Michael C Sparkes
Mark Spear
Michael D Spence
N E Spencer
Colin Spinks
Paul & Janet Stanley
Mr & Mrs P W Stanyer
Dr Brian Stedeford
Mr & Mrs D A Steel
C G & Mrs B R Stone
Dr & Dr H A Stradling
Matthew Strain
Jack Sullivan
Michael & Joan Sweeney
James & Frances Sylvester
Mark Tapping, AIBSA FGSSA
Alexander Taylor
Dr & Mrs D S Taylor
Edwin Taylor
Alexander Taylor
Robert James Taylor
Mr & Mrs A G Tebbutt
George Ashley Tebbutt
Mr J D Tebbutt
Oliver Greville Tebbutt
Peggie Joyce Tetlow

Edgar James Thatcher
Paul, Maureen & Eleanor Thomas
    (In memory of Graham)
Richard M Thomas
Ian James Aird Thompson
Michael Thompson
Sheila Thorogood
Brian Thorpe
John & Jackie Thorpe
Colin & Marianne Thursby
Mrs N E I Tidmarsh
Malcolm Timms
Philip & Dorothy Toler
C P & P A Tomlinson
Prudence Jane Toplis (née Bartlett)
Gerald Tucker
D K O & E Ullmann
Mrs V E Vass
Dr & Mrs A D Vella
Phyllis M Vernon
Elliott Viney
Dr C A Vinson
Michael Walker
Jack James Wallington
Geoffrey Warrington
Joy Waters
Callum Watkinson
Duncan Watkinson
J M Watson; John A Watson;
    A A Watson
P Watson
David & Sheena Watters
Mr & Mrs G A Watts
A Webster
B Webster
C Webster
R J Webster
Dr R Colin Welch
Jack & Doris Wells
Richard & Dorothy Wells
Mr Derek West
Mr & Mrs B Westgate

Doris White
Miss Kathleen E White
Simon Whittington
Mr K Willkinson
Martin & Joanna Wilkinson
Mrs P E Wilkinson
Mr & Mrs P Willdridge
Chris & Di Williams
Mr & Mrs J Williams
Lyn & Jane Williams
Mark & Simon Williams
Martin David Williams
Stephen R Williams
Janet Williamson
Jonathan Williamson
Joan Wills (née Collier)
Keith Wills

Graham & Nicola Wilson
Mr & Mrs J L Wilson
Paul S Wilson
Robert B Wilson
Mr & Mrs S Wilson
E S & A J Wiltshire
Toby Winterbottom
Tom Winterbottom
Alex Winwright
Francis & Gudrun Wood
Nigel Wood
Peter & Anne Worrell
Mrs Gill Wotton
Gill & Graham Wright
Nigel Wright
T Zeldin

Part 1
THE OLD SCHOOL

SIR HENRY LEE AND THE DONATIONS

The founder of Aylesbury Grammar School was Sir Henry Lee of Ditchley (1530-1610). The precise date of the founding of the school is uncertain. Robert Gibbs in his pioneering *History of Aylesbury* (1870) stated that: 'In a correspondence of Sir William Cecil – suggested by Queen Elizabeth herself – on the loss which, as regards the lack of education, has been sustained by all classes through the suppression of the monasteries, the Knight of Quarrendon expressed his readiness to found a free school for Aylesbury youths, a good work of which he first laid the foundation, and subsequently promoted its steady growth and solid interest by two further donations, one in 1598 and another in 1603'. No source is quoted for this information. It does not appear in such correspondence of Sir Henry Lee as is printed in the relevant volumes of the Marquess of Salisbury's Hatfield Manuscripts (1883). Nor is there any reference to the school or to the donations in the *State Papers … left by Sir William Cecil Lord Burghlay* (Samuel Haynes and William Murdin, 2 Vols. London 1740-59). These are the two most likely published sources. Nevertheless, even if there is no confirmation that the commonly accepted date of the foundation of the school is correct, the four hundredth anniversary of the first donation is as good an occasion to celebrate as any. The first school, identified as a Free or Latin School, is said to have been 'in the south-east corner' of St. Mary's Church. The fact that Sir Henry acquired the adjacent Prebendal estate (Hanley 1986) and that Lady Anne, his wife, and two infant sons were buried in the north transept in 1592 would have favoured the establishment of a school in such a setting. There may or may not be any significance in the fact that the first donation followed his installation as the first commoner to be appointed Knight of the Garter in 1597.

Sir Henry Lee of Ditchley was Lord of the Manor of Fleet Marston and Quarrendon and son of Sir Anthony Lee, one of whose 'goodly mansions' was at nearby Burston. His wife Anne, daughter of Lord Paget of West Drayton, was related to Sir William Cecil. They lived at Quarrendon, though in 1579 Sir Henry was given custody under the Great Seal 'of a garden and meadows belonging to the manor of Woodstock' – of which the Royal Manor of Ditchley was a part.

The first letter by Sir Henry bearing the Woodstock address (which is printed in the Hatfield manuscripts) is dated December 1597. By this time, Sir Henry had been formally appointed The Ranger of Woodstock. There is correspondence headed Quaryngeton in April 1593, May 1594 and August 1597, but none contains reference to a school. Sir Henry was back in Quarrendon again in 1598, the year of the first donation. He does not appear to have enjoyed his Oxfordshire 'garden and meadows'. In 1601, he wrote of 'my poor Woodstock cottage' and 'my idle fits in this barren place where seldom anything is good.' In 1603, at the time of the second donation, his address was 'Woodstock Lodge' – an old hunting lodge where he is reported to have installed Anne Vavaseur, his mistress, but correspondence from there refers only to 'a passion of the gout'. It is strange that the name Ditchley does not appear on any of the Cecil correspondence and that little is known of the house at Woodstock itself.

John Leland, who had visited Aylesbury in the days of Sir Henry's youth, commented that it had 'a celebrated market', was 'medley well byldid with tymber' and had *a domus civica* in the market place. It acquired its charter from Queen Mary in 1554. Some years later, William Campden described it as 'pretty populous' and the town was no wit inferior to High Wycombe where the Royal Grammar School was founded in 1562 or to nearby Thame where Lord Williams' School was established in 1559. Aylesbury Grammar School was among some two hundred Latin and Grammar Schools founded by the Crown and other patrons in the sixteenth century following the Reformation under Henry VIII and the Act of 1547 which confiscated all chantries, chapels and religious fraternities. Doubtless, the Lee family had already contributed indirectly if not directly to the instruction of the young before the Reformation, having supported the teaching order of the House of Friars in Aylesbury. Faithful to Queen Elizabeth, they shared in what a later author, Nicholas Carlisle, described as 'the noble impulse in the

The portrait of Sir Henry Lee by Antonio Mor (or Moro) is in the National Portrait Gallery (No. 2095). A similar portrait is in the corridor of the Hall of the Worshipful Company of Armourers and Brasiers.

Founding of Grammar Schools' which was considered as 'one of the Divine means for bringing about the blessed Reformation.'

Sir Henry Lee, who was brought up in this era, belonged to the rising class of gentry and the new breed of English landowners. Campden wrote of 'the vast numbers of well-fleeced sheep' in the Vale of Aylesbury – 'a great profit to their owners'. Sir Henry's flock must have been among the largest. The Quarrendon estate was obviously left in charge of an overseer, because Sir Henry's most active years were spent in London (where an address in the Savoy is recorded). As Knight of the Shire, he attended parliament in 1557-58 and 1571-72. In between he appears to have taken minor diplomatic missions to the continent. He rose to become Knight Marshall and Master of the Leash and organiser of Queen Elizabeth's tournaments and her champion at the Accession Day Tilts. As Sergeant and Master of the Armoury in the Tower of London and Keeper of the Armour and other Habiliments of War in or near 'le Tylteyearde' in Greenwich, he would have been responsible for the testing of weapons.

It was natural that he should become a Master of the Worshipful Company of Armourers and Brasiers. His status was such that he was honoured by a two day visit at Quarrendon by 'his Royal Mistress during her progresses and public processions' in 1592 (Nichols p. 125), when a masque was performed (ibid. p. 195). Later, James I and his Queen are reported to have visited Woodstock.

Sir Henry Lee was born in 1530 and died without a male heir at Spelsbury in Oxfordshire. The church records of Bierton give the date of death as February 12, 1610. He was buried in St. Peter's church in Quarrendon, a chapel of ease of St. James's church at Bierton. The elaborate memorial that was erected to him is described in several sources (Bickersteth. 1863). The Quarrendon estate passed out of the Lee family in 1787. In 1817, St. Peter's Chapel was described as 'a melancholy object of contemplation' from which the numerous memorials had long since disappeared.

All of the known portraits of Sir Henry Lee are listed under his name in the Catalogues of the Library of the National Portrait Gallery (cf also Roe 1942). The three best may be mentioned. The portrait by Marcus Gheeraedhs the Younger is probably the finest. It is in the Armourer's Hall of the Tower of London (Frontispiece). What appears to have been a copy, presented by the Rev. F.G. Lee in 1891 hung in the school hall until the fire of 1953. The second best-known portrait is by Antonio Mor (or Moro). It is dated 1568 and is in the possession of the National Portrait Gallery. A copy hangs in the school staff room. The third portrait of consequence is of Sir Henry Lee in his Garter robes. It is also by Marcus Gheeraedhs and is dated 1602. It is in the hall of the Worshipful

Company of Armourers and Brasiers. Hanging beside it is a full-length portrait of Lady Anne Vavaseur – according to one discreet epithet 'the dulcinea of Sir Henry'. Sir Henry's suit of armour, made in the royal workshops at Greenwich by Jacob Halder, is also in the possession of the Livery Company.

The original endowment of Aylesbury Grammar School, 'of the reported value of eight pounds only', is described by Robert Gibbs as consisting of 'two messuages vested in certain trustees, of whom the Vicar of Aylesbury appears to have been one.' The schoolmaster was probably paid partly by the receipt of rents from the houses and partly from payment by the boys. According to a report of the Charity Commissioners, (1815-34 p. 576) he taught 'by licence from the vicar in a room adjoining and belonging to the church, which is supposed formerly to have been a chantry chapel' (which would have become redundant following the Reformation). `The original trustees under the will were listed by Gibbs as the Rev. T. Lodington (Vicar of Aylesbury, d. 1728), William Church Esq., Paul Heywood Esq., and Joseph Bell Esq. Gibbs also refers to a rent of two pounds a year from a tenement and lands in the city of Canterbury from a 'collateral of Sir Henry', Sir Richard Lee, but this was later lost. There are no known records from the seventeenth century. According to a report received from the school by Nicholas Carlisle (1818), 'The writings of the original school endowment are supposed to have been lost in the Civil Wars'. However, it may be assumed that Aylesbury Grammar School conformed to the situation described in Christopher Wase, 'Considerations concerning Free Schools as settled in England' (1678). Until the end of the Commonwealth 'the material of instruction was exclusively classical.' The number of post-Reformation primers in Latin multiplied rapidly (Watson, 1968). Writing schools were slow to increase. Four schoolmasters are mentioned by Gibbs (p. 477) from 1678 with the Rev. Ralph Gladman who was appointed in 1692 continuing as the first head of the new school. In the Ecclesiastical Visitation to the Wendover deanery in 1709, reference was made to the schoolmaster, Ralph Gladman having 'a house and about twenty scholars'. (Broad, p. 222). It was a modest provision for a town of 500 families. The situation was changed fundamentally by the bequest of Henry Phillips.

PHILLIPS' GIFT

The will of Henry Phillips, gentleman of London, was granted probate (in Latin) on November 24, 1714 old style 'in the prerogative court of the Archbishop of Canterbury'. The bequest of £5,000 substantially increased the endowment of Sir Henry Lee. The bequest was made on trust to Henry Phillips' cousins William and John Mead, members of a somewhat prolific family from Mursley who were also beneficiaries. William, who seems to have owned the Manor of Broughton (VCH II p. 324) and who rebuilt The Prebendal in 1710, was 'a member and assistant' of the Dyers Company (Hanley p. 37). He was High Sheriff for Buckinghamshire in 1716. John, who was described as a citizen and grocer of London, died in 1718.

Curiously little is known about Henry Phillips. Aylesbury was 'the place of his nativity'. He was born on September 14, 1640 and died at the age of 75. His father had been a Justice of the Peace and a 'linen draper' by trade. In the *Observation* on a *Brief* attributed to Messrs. White, Eyre and White of Bedford Row, London (B.R.O./CH3/L2/14), 'Mr. Phillips is supposed to have been a dissenter'. In fact, there were a considerable number of dissenting families in Aylesbury. The 1709 visitation recording 'Quakers, Presbyterians and Anabaptists, many' (Broad p. 222). 'It is clear', the *Brief* continues, 'that he incurred the displeasure of the restored government for his conduct during the Commonwealth, although he afterwards obtained a pardon which is still extant among the documents belonging to the school'. According to the will, he wished to be interred in the chancel of Aylesbury church. It was considered to be an unsuitable place for a dissenter (the writer of the *Brief* continued), 'but he might have been ambitious of notoriety and thought the church a more public place for a monument'. In fact, in the will, Phillips' request was to be buried 'as near the place where my late father is buried as convenient'. (B.R.O./CH3/E3/25). A mural monument was placed in his honour.

By the terms of the will, the sum upon trust was to be applied 'for the purchase of lands of inheritance in fee simple in the county of Bucks or as near to the same as conveniently might be, to be settled by his executors,

A photograph of the portrait of Henry Phillips which used to hang in the school hall but which was destroyed in the fire of 1953. Its provenance is unknown, but it would seem to have been in the possession of the school before 1890.

or the survivor of them, upon trustees in succession for ever, for the enlargement of and further provision for the Free School in Aylesbury, for instructing poor boys of Aylesbury and Walton in the first place from time

The mural monument to Henry Phillips in the vestry of St. Mary's Church, Aylesbury.

NEAR
this Place lie the Bodies of
MATTHIAS DAGNALL Bookseller
and SARAH his Wife,
She Died Aug.st 23. 1736. Aged 76 Years.
He Died Sept 26. 1736. Aged 78 Years.
And also their Sons MATTHIAS and
DEVERELL DAGNALL with ALICE and
ELIZABETH their Wives,
MATTHIAS Died April. 8. 1773. Aged. 76.
DEVERELL Died Dec. 7. 1773. Aged. 74.
DEVERELL his Son Died Jan.ry 13. 1776. Aged. 29.
ELIZABETH Wife of DEVERELL Died Aug.st 18.
1784. Aged. 59.
ALICE Wife of MATTHIAS Died Oct.r 18.
1786. Aged. 75.
Also THOMAS DAGNALL Bookseller
Son of MATTHIAS and ALICE
He Died Dec.r 12. 1792. Aged. 46.
JOHN PARKER Gent. died Dec.r 31. 1811.
aged 63 Years,
ELIZABETH, Daughter of DEVERELL & ELIZth
DAGNALL died June 1st 1817. aged 73 Years,
ANN Widow first of Thos. DAGNALL afterwards of
JOHN PARKER died March 22.d 1819, aged 72 Years
MARY, Wife of A.P. MUDDIMAN and Daughter
of DEVERELL and ELIZth DAGNALL died Oct.r 10th
1834. aged 77 Years.

ALEXANDER PHILLIPS MUDDIMAN,
DIED 30.t DECEMBER 1855.
AGED 77 YEARS.

The mural monument to Matthias Dagnall, the man in charge of the building of the school, is in the Lady Chapel.

9

to time for ever, for providing sufficient and convenient books and other necessaries for that purpose; and for want of a sufficient number of poor boys in the said parishes of Aylesbury and Walton ... or the instructing of other such poor boys from the next neighbouring parishes.'

Some £4,000 of the bequest was speedily invested in farm property in the Manor of Broughton ('alias Broughton Abbotts alias Abbotts Broughton in the parish of Byerton alias Bierton' which had belonged to Missenden Abbey before the Dissolution). The property consisted of the Manor Farm, including a mill and land between Bierton and Stock Lake. Most of the land was held in 'close pieces'. All of the individual fields and closes were named – Mill Meadow, Cow Mead, Bushey Close, College Mead, Inner Moor, Outer Moor, and a pasture ground known as Stock Lake. Some strips were also held in open field. The inheritance of the land was invested in the trustees in the first instance for 'a term of 500 years'. *The Abstract of the Deed of Entitlement* was dated March 31, 1715.

Ten Trustees were appointed by the High Court of Chancery in 1717, together with one trustee from the old charity. There was a stipulation in the will that in the event of disagreements among the trustees concerning the school, the monies should be used for the erection of almshouses. It is recorded that four of the old trustees 'were continually cavilling and setting themselves in opposition to the said William Mead'. The chief point of disagreement appears to have been the delay in providing a new school building. There was even reference to the almshouses. But the defence, which was upheld, was that no time limit had been set for the erection of the school buildings. The words of the will were 'as soon as may be conveniently after my decease'. The old school was described twice in the Court of Chancery report (B.R.O./CH3/L/9). It was first listed as a room adjacent to the church ' ... the which by negligence of the trustees was wasted for want of repairs.' Secondly, it was identified as 'a schoolroom adjoining the church where a Grammar School was kept and which belonged to the church being always repaired by the churchwardens and the schoolmaster there teached by lycence from the parson under no obligation to teach gratis ... (he) had heard that in the Civil Wars the writings which were title to the premises were lost'.

It is not surprising that in the High Court document it was stated that 'if it should be found that the present room cannot be made capable for the reception of boys without incommoding the church', then it would be necessary 'to find some other fit place for the building of the new school.' It was also required that there should be an inscription on the new school to the effect that 'this school was originally founded by Sir Henry Leigh of Ditchley and since more enlarged and more amply provided and made a Free School by Henry Phillips gent. of London.'

The High Court was anxious that 'as a result of the size of the new bequest the original charity should not be swallowed up and the name of the first founder lost'. By a degree of the Court of Chancery dated February 4, 1720 the following rules and ordinances were established:

1. 'There shall be 120 boys admitted into the said school, to be taught gratis, and to be furnished with books, pens, ink, and paper, gratis.'

2. 'There shall be appointed one schoolmaster and one usher for teaching the said boys in reading English, Latin and Greek; and also one writing-master for teaching and instructing the said boys in writing and accounts; the which said schoolmaster and usher, and also the writing-master, shall attend their respective duties in the said school at least ten hours in every week day, not being holydays.'

3. 'Relates to the appointment and dismissal of schoolmasters.'

4. 'Gives a power to the trustees to perform or not, at their discretion, at any time within two years, certain acts which they had not performed.'

5. 'Upon the death or removal of any one of of the said trustees, the trustees or the major part of them shall nominate some other person or persons to be trustee or trustees in the room of him or them so dead or removed; and as often as the present trustees, or any subsequent trustees, shall by death or otherwise be reduced to five in number, the survivors of such trustees shall convey the estate to the other trustees, who shall be so nominated in the room of those that die or remove.'

6. 'The schoolmaster and usher for the time being shall take care that the said boys do come to school on every school day, from

Lady-day to Michaelmas-day in every year, at six o'clock in the morning and there remain till eleven o'clock in the forenoon, and do come again at one o'clock in the afternoon and there remain till six o'clock; and from Michaelmas-day to Lady-day, the said boys do attend at school from seven o'clock till eleven in the forenoon and from one till five in the afternoon.'

7.   'The schoolmaster and usher, and writing-master, in respect of the teaching the said 120 boys, shall not on any account whatsoever receive any gift, present, or other matter or thing of or from any of the said boys, or of or from any of their parents or friends, but shall have and receive from the said trustees such salaries respectively as they the said trustees shall see convenient.'

8.   'The schoolmaster for the time being shall and may receive and teach in the said school, for his own profit and advantage, in Latin, Greek and Hebrew only, so many other scholars, the sons of wealthy and substantial parents, as the said school shall be capable to receive, not exceeding twenty in number, and so as the boys to be taught gratis shall not be prejudiced or neglected thereby.'

Effectively this implied the establishment of two schools – the Free School proper and a group of fee-paying pupils who were to be taught the classics only. As the years passed a distinction grew between the so-called Lower School and the Latin School, though the latter was by no means confined to fee-paying pupils.

The new school premises were formally conveyed to the trustees by 'indentures of lease and release dated 13th and 14th September 1737' (Gibbs p. 479)

BUILDING THE OLD SCHOOL

The premises to be occupied by the Free School and the master's house were built between 1718 and 1720 on Broad Street, which later became Church Street. It would appear that part of an earlier building was incorporated in the new structure (J.C. Trench and P. Fenley p. 26-32) The new buildings were erected at a cost of £1,267/18/2 on the site of 'two ancient messuages which formed the property of the old charity' (Gibbs p. 478). The details were recorded in the *Accounts of Mr. Mead of the Rents and Profits of the Estate at Broughton* (B.R.O./CH3/F4/1/1). The receipts derived from rents paid by the first tenants – Mrs. Amy Jordan, Mrs. Mary Cross and Mr. George Moller – were also recorded.

The principal outgoings were paid to Mr. Matthias Dagnall who was described as 'the Aylesbury stationer and bookseller', though he would also appear to have been something of a building contractor. (There is a mural monument to him and his family in St. Mary's Church.) Payments began in 1718 and continued monthly during the building period until January 1720. There were separate payments for the transport of timber and other materials. The *Account for Mr. Mead of building the Free School. Per contra disbursements for the by order of Mr. Mead* (B.R.O./CH3/FA/1/1) lists weekly sums paid to individual labourers. In July 1718, some twenty workmen were employed, thereafter the numbers were between ten and twenty, dropping to four or five at the beginning and end of the building season. The average wage was about a shilling a day, variations in pay probably reflecting individual skills. Thus, David Horn received 4/6 for 1½ days work and William Hailey 7/4 for four days work. The roll call of names is typical for mid- Buckinghamshire. The total weekly payments for the working year 1718 varied from £10/6/6 for the week of August 22 to £1/0/5 for the week of October 8. Payments for the carriage of materials were very precisely signed 'of Wm. Mead, Esq., by the hand of Matthias Dagnall.' Materials consisted principally of timber, bricks (from the many small kilns in the neighbourhood), lime (the best known local kilns were in the Ivinghoe area), stonework (from Headington near Oxford) and sand (from the Wing area). When the outer structure was nearing completion, other products were required – 136 feet of oak boards (expert sawyers appear on the accounts in this context, with payments for 450 and 960 feet of sawing). Next came door cases, turned goods and other carpenter's products. A pump was bought for the well. Finally came plumbing and glazing bills – expensive in the context of other disbursements – £100 between October 1719 and March 1720.

William Mead, the senior trustee, died in 1724 leaving the school

£100 in his will. It was the equivalent of payment for 2,000 working days of a labourer at 1/- an hour or just about the cost of glazing and plumbing.

Estimate of the charge for the erecting of a school house and houses for the schoolmasters for the Free School in Aylesbury

	£	s.	d.
44 Rod of brickwork at £7 per rod	308	00	00
46 square of tiling at 20 shillings a square	46	00	00
472 yards of ceiling at 12d a yard	23	12	00
1300 yards of rendering at 6d a yard	33	08	00
46Ω rod of mound wall brick	45	10	00
For timber boards and carpenter's work	450	00	00
For lead and plumber's work	45	00	00
For iron work and nails	30	00	00
For locks and latches	2	00	00
Colouring windows and doors	3	12	00
Glazing	36	15	00
Stone paving	20	00	00
Brick paving	8	17	06
Digging cellars and carrying away rubbish	6	00	00
Out offices	42	00	00
	£1,100	14	06
To be deducted for the old houses	60	00	00
	£1,040	14	06

ORDERING THE FREE SCHOOL

When the trustees held their first meeting on October 1, 1720, they had in their possession the Decree of the High Court of Chancery of February 4, 1720 containing the rules and ordinances for the government of the school. Thereafter, the trustees agreed to meet annually on March 14 and September 14 'which date was the birthday of Mr. Henry Phillips, the benefactor' (B.R.O./CH3/AM1).

Appointments, salaries, additional regulations and matters appertaining to the property at Broughton were to be recorded by the writing master in *The Orders and Agreements of the Trustees* (B.R.O./CH3/AG/1). He was 'to be allowed five pounds for keeping and examining the accounts of the trustees'. One of the first acts of the trustees was to order a stone with the description required by the Court of Chancery. The Rev. Ralph Gladman, who had been a schoolmaster since 1687, and who took the oath of allegiance as schoolmaster two years later, continued in office under the new dispensation. His usher was 'discharged … for his immoraility' in 1720. Gladman retired with a pension of £20 in 1725. In his will, proved Aylesbury 1725 (B.R.O. Ms. Wills peculiar 25/5/30), he bequeathed his books relating to 'grammar and school learning' to 'Ye Grammar School' and his books on divinity to be left there for the use of poor clergy. Locks were bought by the trustees 'to keep them from damage.'

Gladman was succeeded by the Rev. William Mason, who became master of the Latin School at an annual salary of £45. For some reason it was considered necessary to advise Mr. Mason that he should 'daily and constantly attend the school'. Francis North became the writing master at £40 p.a. and John Boughton, an assistant at £25. By a special resolution, John Boughton was to be allowed 'ten pounds augmentation to his salary in consideration of his being a relation to the donor of the school,' but he was forbidden to give instruction without the order of the writing master. A Mr. Eggleton was to have forty shillings a year for ringing the school bell at appropriate times of the day. In 1742, presumably following Eggleton's death, the sexton took over at a cheaper rate. The Chancery Decree having omitted reference to 'the age of the poor children to be admitted', it was agreed that it should be 'five years provided they can read'.

The rules of the school were extended to make provision for the correction of 'such boys as shall fight or quarrel with any school fellows'. Not more than two boys were to be allowed 'to go out for any end or under any pretence whatsoever.' The Master was required 'to set from time to time … and order the boys to do exercises at home and show them to him the following morning.' The catechism was to be heard 'once a week in Greek, Latin … and English … according to the capacities of the scholars.' All such boys as were not dissenters (should) constantly repair to church as often as there shall be publick prayers and

June 3d 1719 Received of William Mead Esqr by the
hands of Matthias Dagnall Ten pounds for Brick &
Lime for the School I say received   10-0-0

Witness with Grassum   by me   The mark of
                                Charles [☐] Durvall

June the 5th   To the Workmen

To Richard Sims for 5 days at 20d pr day ——   0-8-4
Thomas Sims for 6 days at 8d pr day ——   0-4-0
Nicholas Sims for 4 days & half at 6d pr day — 0-2-3
Edward Clark for 6 days at 20d pr day ——   0-10-0
Nicholas Sims Middle man for 6 days at 20d pr day — 0-10-0
John Butler for 6 days at 20d pr day ——   0-10-0
William Willgoss for 4 days at 20d pr day ——   0-6-8
Richard Willgoss for 4 days at 8d pr day ——   0-2-8
William Healy for 5 days at 20d pr day —   0-8-4
Rich Healy for 5 days at 9d pr day —   0-3-9
Thos Brafter for 3 days at 20d pr day —   0-5-0
John Clark for 4 days at 18d pr day ——   0-6-0
John Walton for 4 days & ½ at 12d pr day —   0-4-6
Thomas Walton for 5 days & ½ at 12d pr day —   0-5-5
Joseph Whitchunk for 6 days at 12d pr day —   0-6-0
Francis Wallis for 6 days at 12d pr day —   0-6-0
Thomas Money for 6 days at 12d pr day —   0-6-0
John Molloy for 3 days at 12d pr day ——   0-3-0
John Tegg for 2 days at 12d pr day —   0-2-0
Richard Chargr for Sawing 650 foot ——   0-19-6
                                                 —————
                                                  6 9-6

June 6th 1719 Received of William Mead Esqr by
the hands of Matthias Dagnall four pounds thirteen 4-13-0
Shillings in full for hair for the use of William Rough
I say received
              by me   Jeffery Smith

that they (should) behave decently and orderly whilst there. Furthermore for the encouragement of the boys, those 'who had learned fastest (should) be placed together in the school' and together 'in the seats at the church than with the more negligent boys.'

Already by the time that the property had been formally made over to the trustees in 1737, a new writing master, James Neale, had been appointed. He was to serve under the Rev. John Stephens ('a very corpulent man') who had been curate in Aylesbury since 1736 and who succeeded the Rev. William Mason in 1744. School numbers were increasing. In 1745, there were 96 'writers', 50 'readers' and twelve in the Grammar School. Among other tasks, James Neale was responsible for notifying the trustees fourteen days before the date of each meeting and arranging for them to have dinner (at a cost of about £2 on the school account). Meetings appear to have been held at The White Hart, The Queen's Head and The George in Aylesbury.

On these occasions, the accounts were agreed and new trustees were appointed as required. John Wilkes, who later acquired great notoriety for his radical activities, became a trustee on August 1, 1748. He was a friend of John Stephens, lived at The Prebendal at the time and became the local Member of Parliament. He was the subject of a number of libellous attacks. One of them was set to the tune of a popular song *The Dragon of Wantley*:

> But the Aylesbury men like fools
> Thought John Wilkes a great rarity.
> They made him trustee of the schools,
> But he swallowed up the charity.

There is no evidence in the trustees' minutes that this controversial figure was guilty of any impropriety during the short period that he held office. He signed the accounts as a trustee on several occasions. Technically, he remained in office until 1797 but his name soon disappeared from among those attending.

After the demise of John Stephens, the Reverend William Pugh, a curate of Aylesbury and chaplain to the County Gaol, took over the Latin mastership. In turn, he was succeeded three years later in 1774 by the

Reverend William Stockins. Stockins was a native of Aylesbury who had 'received grammatical instruction in the school itself' before he went to Jesus College Oxford. Having promised that 'he would not accept the chaplaincy of the Aylesbury gaol' he subsequently contrived to function as Vicar of Stone and Domestic Chaplain to Sir William Lee at Hartwell as well as instructing pupils privately. He was described by one pupil as an 'amiable and excellent teacher' (Lipscomb, II, p. 65). He was to remain as headmaster for some thirty years. During his regime, it was agreed that the terms of Henry Phillips' will should be brought before the trustees and additional rules be approved (Minute Book, Trustees B.R.O./CH3/M). Among other items, it was agreed that a teacher could be removed for neglect of duty by a two-thirds majority of the trustees. In fact, the first dismissal of a master was for 'financial irregularities' in 1801.

Reference to repairs to the school buildings by William Dagnall (son of Matthias) began in 1754. Sun Fire Insurance entered the books in 1755. The accumulated income was sufficient in 1774 to acquire £150 of stock in South Sea Old Annuities (They were sold in 1801). More stock was purchased in 1784-85 and in 1805.

It is possible that about this time George Lipscomb (1773-1846), author of the three volume *History and Antiquities of the County of Buckingham* (1847), was among the boys at the school. The *Dictionary of National Biography* refers to him being educated at Quainton and Aylesbury before he went to St. Bartholomew's Hospital. John Bonnycastle (1750-1821), born in Whitchurch, was also at the school (Carlisle, 1818). He was an eminent mathematician who also published a large number of text-books on arithmetic.

By the end of the century, the school was showing increasing signs of wear and tear. The coping on the main building, the scullery roof, and the brewhouse floor all needed attention (25/3/1780). A complaint was received from a churchwarden (28/3/1795) 'that the Latin School was very much out of repair and dangerous for the master and scholars.' Yorkshire stone for repairs to the kitchen and passage of the school house was called for (18/9/1814). The following year there was reference to 'a new privy built for the boys' (31/10/1815) and 'a drain from the necessary to the common sewer.' Plumbing and glazing were required (1816).

The headmasters, not least as clerks in holy orders, were continuously dependent upon patronage for their livings. William Stockins was a Whig and his successor, the Rev. John Rawbone (a former pupil of the school) who was appointed in 1806, was of the same persuasion. Other activities may well have led to the neglect of his headmasterly responsibilities. The services of the usher Joseph Wynne were dispensed with (he was allowed £15). Thomas de Fraine and John Hilliard remained in post, with salaries of £80 and £100 respectively; but Thomas de Fraine was soon the subject of complaints. The Rev. John Rawbone resigned in 1813 and William Stockins stepped into the breach until 1817 when the trustees appointed the Rev. Charles Robert Ashfield at a salary of £170 plus his residence.

Meanwhile, the townsfolk of Aylesbury were beginning to express

A sketch of the school seen from the churchyard as it was in the mid-nineteenth century.

dissatisfaction with the school. The first of a series of complaints was voiced in 1813 – 'the school is not well conducted in consequence of the incapacity of the masters through age, infirmity and other causes' (6/3/1813). The school was evidently considered at a meeting held on that date at the home of Viscount Hampden in London. In addition to Viscount Hampden the body of trustees at that time was impressive. They included Lord Cavendish, The Duke of Portland, Sir John Dashwood-King, (who took over the vacancy caused by the departure of John Wilkes), Robert Greenhill, Thomas Tyrwhitt Drake, the Rev. Henry Millner and Mr. G.R. Minshull. Perhaps most of them were too busy with other matters to pay more than lip service to the office of trustee though they did discuss the renewal of the inscription to the founders of the school (black marble with gold letters). It is interesting to think of their journeys to the school house, with post-chaises arriving in Broad Street from half a dozen different estates, for 10.00 a.m. meetings with Sir John the new chairman resident at Halton.

The accounts begin to show the concern of the trustees about taxes. They agreed with some reluctance to pay the window taxes of John Rawbone, but Charles Ashfield was required to pay all the rates and taxes on his residence. A land tax of £1.8.0 was payable by the trustees to the parish of Aylesbury in the 1820s, while a reply from the 'Office of Taxes' (4/1/1804) indicated that unlike hospitals and alms houses, 'the lodging, clothing and diet of scholars...was not exempt from duty.'

A tightening of discipline followed the appointment of the new Headmaster. Dismissals for irregularity of attendance by the scholars were introduced. The Headmaster reported the names of those admitted and dismissed at each meeting of the trustees. Fifteen boys were dismissed (31/10/1815) for absence exceeding fifty days. Perhaps in order to strengthen morale, all boys were required to attend divine worship collectively on Sundays. More books were acquired – twenty Bibles and 'some abridgements of history.' In 1815, the first 'awards for merit' were made in the shape of books 'of morals and religious tracts.'

The matter of boarders – presumably fee-paying pupils – was seriously discussed for the first time (10/5/1819). It was noted that the premises would have to be made suitable for them, 'but they would increase the respectability of the school'. At the same time there was disquiet about Mr. de Fraine's inefficiency 'on account of the new system of teaching'. It prompted action by the townsfolk, and the trustees had to receive a deputation (21/8/1821) 'representing their objections to the Bell system of teaching.' De Fraine was pensioned off, having admitted his incompetence.

The minutes suggest that a measure of financial stress was beginning to affect the school. In 1825, it was decided that 'the salaries of the masters be reduced in consequence of the insufficiency of funds.' The situation was only partly eased by discontinuing the pension paid to Joseph Wynne (who was suspected of perpetrating a criminal act). Simultaneously, there was a further tightening of attendance at school. Ten days absence would result in dismissal and entry was to be refused to boys 'who were not clean in their person or properly dressed' (24/9/1825).

The next time a new headmaster was appointed, an advertisement was placed in Oxford, Cambridge and Buckinghamshire newspapers (3/10/1829). Four clerical gentlemen applied. The Rev. Benjamin Robert Perkins was appointed. He immediately demanded that 'books of reference and maps be obtained...since the boys do not supply themselves with books.' He also reported that he 'could not occupy a house so wanting in convenience and comfort' and sought permission to live in the town. No doubt this was partly a result of the action of his predecessor, the Rev. Mr. Ashfield, who was reported as having taken certain fixtures from the house, thereby causing 'great dilapidations and mutilations.' Accordingly, not for the first time, the headmaster was non-resident, choosing to live at Cublington, some seven miles away, where he also served as curate. The Rev. Benjamin Perkins never succeeded in stimulating the musical life of the school as he had hoped (14/1/1831), but on relinquishing his post in 1835 to the Rev. John Grant Lawford, he made a bequest of books to the school (a key had to be acquired to lock them up). And Mr. Field provided 'a new timekeeper' for the sum of seven pounds. During Perkins' regime, the Report of the Commissioners concerning Charities and Education, 1815-34, stated that the school 'affords incontestible evidence of judicious management'. Such was the inheritance of the Rev. John Lawford who was to retire in 1840.

'DEVIATIONS FROM THE REGULATIONS'

By the 1830s a national interest in education was awakening and an Education Committee of the Privy Council was established. In the following decade, there were significant local developments in Aylesbury. A British School was established in 1844: and a National School shortly after. Both were supported from charitable sources. A Mechanics Institute was founded in 1848, which Dr. Lee of Hartwell had helped to endow. Dr. Lee, a polymath of considerable repute and an active patron of education elsewhere, never appears to have had the slightest contact with the Free School.

In 1846, an attempt had been made by a group of townsfolk to seek an interview with the trustees, but there had been no acknowledgement of their memorial – nor is there any mention of it in the *Minute Book of the Trustees* for the year. The general expression of dissatisfaction with the management and condition of the Free School found another expression through the British and National Schools. The Free School immediately lost a full quarter of its pupils. It had been noted in 1843, that among the hundred boys in the Lower School, 59 were dissenters. The following year there were 96 boys. In 1846, the figure fell to 69. It was reported that twelve had left for the National School and five for the British School.

The dissenters were a relatively strong group among 'the 6,000 souls' of mid-nineteenth century Aylesbury. Some were also relatively wealthy and influential, as the non-conformist chapels that they and their immediate descendants built attest. Among others, they numbered the highly articulate Robert Gibbs, the radical editor of *The Bucks Advertiser and Aylesbury News,* and his father John Gibbs, who had attended the school as a boy. On February 3, 1849, a letter was published in the *Advertiser* in which twenty questions were asked about 'the Latin and Grammar School.' It was signed by Queriest who contributed a second letter on March 3 about some of the answers that he had received. The discontent was such that at first 2½ columns were devoted to the school's situation (7/4/1849) and then another 2½ (14/4/1849). A leading article followed demanding that 'the town's education' be rescued from 'barrenness and sterility' and that it should

Robert Gibbs (1816-93), whose father John Gibbs founded the Aylesbury Advertiser in 1836 and was a pupil at the school, played a significant part in the deliberations concerning the state of the school in the mid-nineteenth century.

receive nothing less than 'intellectual regeneration.' On April 23, a large meeting was held in the County Hall. It lasted for three hours and the *Advertiser* reported the unhappy occasion in no less than six columns. Both the trustees (who appeared to treat the Charity as no more than 'a patronage') and the teaching staff were admonished. The Rev. Mr. Cox, headmaster and 'the perpetual curate of Winchendon', was held to be culpable. The gathering appointed a committee under the chairmanship of the Vicar of Aylesbury to devise measures 'to redeem the school from the state of inefficiency into which it had fallen.' Lord Nugent, one of Aylesbury's MPs, was in attendance. Butterworth's *Memorial* was the initial response (CH3/AG/2/1). This was a document some four feet by two feet in size, written in a large copperplate script, which was signed by most of the town's substantial residents. The general memorial presented to the trustees concluded:

> 'We beg to remind the Trustees that this is not the first time that an attempt has been made by inhabitants of this town to call your attention to the existing evils, with a view to their removal, and that a deputation of ourselves, which three years since waited upon you for this purpose, were neither granted an interview nor received any attention to the memorial which they then forwarded to you.
>
> We, therefore, your memorialists, do now hereby call upon you, as being primarily responsible for the due management of this institution, to rectify these serious deviations from the regulations laid down both by the Founder's Will and by the Decree of the Court of Chancery, and to supply these ruinous defects in the administration of the school, in order that the middle and poorer classes in this parish may enjoy that advantage which the well-directed munificence of former days intended for their benefit in the solid and liberal education of their children. And we make this appeal to you in the belief and hope that much as the efficiency and utility of this school have now for many years been impaired under the existing system of management, you will not be indisposed to revert to a beneficial execution of your important trust, at the instance of this public representation and complaint from the inhabitants of this town, who have greatly suffered, for some years past, from the neglected and decayed condition of their Free School, and many of whom, failing to obtain for their children the advantages which they considered themselves as entitled to find in that school, have been compelled, to their cost and inconvenience, to supply this need in other ways.
>
> And we would respectfully intimate to you that we at present

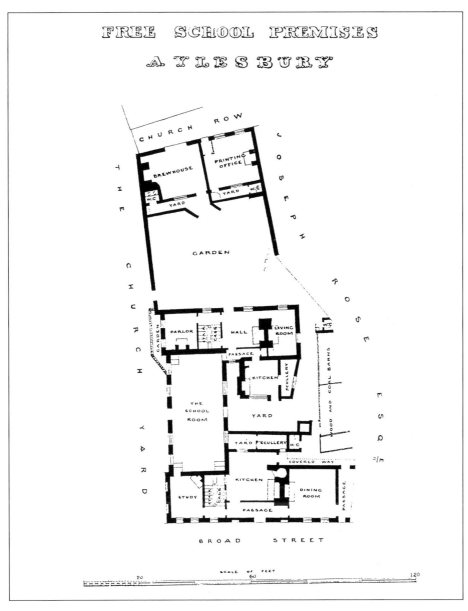

The plan of the school, 1852 from Aylesbury Free School Property – a bound volume among other school documents kept by Messrs. Horwood and James. Its preparation would appear to have been a consequence of the petitions of 1849-50. Residential facilities for the masters and their families seem to have taken precedence over teaching accommodation.

forbear to seek a remedy for the evils of which we complain by requesting our Representatives in Parliament to move for the introduction of a clause meeting our case in a Bill for the Regulation of Charitable Trusts now before the House of Commons, in the sole confidence that you will not reject this, our reasonable request, in consideration of the responsibility and obligations voluntarily assumed by you in accepting the office of Trustees.

In conclusion, we respectfully request you to name as early a day as may be convenient to you for receiving a deputation of inhabitants appointed at this meeting, to lay before you the resolutions passed at it on the subject of the Free School, with such further explanations of the wishes of the inhabitants as may be thought requisite, and to receive your answer to the present memorial'.

At the meeting held in the school house on May 15, 1849, a deputation of eighteen Aylesburians representing some 182 townsfolk was received by the trustees with Lord Carrington, Lord Lieutenant of Buckinghamshire and a liberal in politics, in the chair. The complaints were manifold – the general conduct and attainments of the pupils, the inefficiency of the teaching staff, the methods of teaching, the accommodation, the impossibility of finding out what resources the trustees held. Witnesses were called. Boys, former pupils, parents and others – all from John Gibbs' 'middling classes' – gave evidence, not least on certain Dickensian practices which took place in the school house. Neighbours whose properties were adjacent to the school complained about carpet and mat beating by pupils in the churchyard. Boys gave evidence that they had carried water for the school staff. Knives and forks had been cleaned: also boots and shoes. Errands had been run in school time to shops in the town and to the post office. Stockings and handkerchieves had been washed.

George Cooper claimed that he had 'washed Mr. Heyward's stockings'. 'Sometimes I used to be washing all day' declared a former 'pay boy' styled as Mr. Dupre. The school yard had also been cleaned. Other former pupils – George Bury (innkeeper), Thomas Fell (coal merchant) and George Walton (clockmaker) – who had been at the school for five or more years, confirmed these unsatisfactory practices. They also reported that, in addition to Mr. Heyward, the older boys acted as teachers for the younger boys. All of the older boys expected – or extracted – bribes from the younger pupils. If apples, marbles or peg tops were not forthcoming there might be persecution or punishment (CH3/E1/4). There were worse places. Eton was noted for its squalor and brutality and even Dr. Arnold at Rugby declared himself unable to produce 'Christian gentlemen' out of boys still at school.

A leader written in *The Bucks Advertiser and Aylesbury News* (19/5/1849) had a field day describing 'The Free School Inquisition.' The scene was worthy of an engraving by George Cruikshank. Lord Carrington vowed at the outset of the meeting that he was prepared to listen until midnight if need be. The table at which he sat 'groaned beneath the weight of documents'. As if he were the Prime Minister 'at a cabinet meeting', he had a shorthand clerk beside him 'a messenger of light'. As for the two 'culprits', the Reverend Mr. Cox displayed 'a temper as unruffled and unreverend as possible', while Mr. Heyward looked 'lymphatic'. Mr. Heyward denied his pupils' charges – 'Recriminations would be unworthy'. His submission was on quarto-sized paper, written in a large and not especially legible hand – certainly not one befitting a Writing Master.

Six months later, the anonymous leader writer was still chastising the trustees as 'slumbering enemies of the public good.' In December 1849, the activist Edward Green of Brook Cottage wrote to the solicitors Parrott and Rose asking that a public examination of the boys be set in motion. There was a fair amount of prevarication. The reply accepted that 'to a certain extent' the presence of an inspector should be sufficient to satisfy the townsfolk. A dozen letters were printed on the subject (11/1/1850). Two weeks later, the petitioners were advised that 'HM Inspector has been permitted by the Council of Education to examine the schools.' He would be prepared, however, to hear opinions expressed by other persons. Such 'secrecy' irritated the press. The result was that two days before the inspection, the petitioners were told that the inspector (Mr. F.C. Cook) 'would not have any objection to their presence.' Five townsfolk attended the examination. As for the inspector's report, it was restricted to the President of the Council and the Chairman

Dates of Admission.	NAMES OF BOYS.	Ages of Boys.	NAMES OF PARENTS OR GUARDIANS.
1844			
April 10.	John Tossop	7	William W. Sharp
Sept. 30. 1845	Wm Hall	6	Richard Hall
Dec. 1. "	Robert Bennick	7	Richard Bennick
May 25. 1846	George Bunce	6	William Bunce
Oct. 19. "	Willm Bowden	6	John Bowden
April 1. 1847	Robert Bailey	7	Joseph Bailey
" 12. "	Arthur Reader	5	Henry Reader
May 10. "	John Holloway	5	Joseph Holloway
" "	Emanuel Towersey	6	William Towersey
Augt. 16. "	Richard Barnaby	9	John Barnaby
" "	Willm Barnaby	7	Do
Novr. 17 "	James Bryan	9	widow Bryan
Decr. 3. "	George Evett	6	John Evett
Aug. 11. 1848.	Charles Fell	13	Thomas Fell
Octr. 2. "	James Cornaby	10	James Cornaby
" "	Thos. Grimsdell	7	Henry Grimsdell
Novr. 11. "	Thomas Evett	6	John Evett
Feb. 19. 1849	Thos. Markham	6	Thos. Markham
March 26. "	John Elliman	9	Henry Elliman
" " "	Wm Elliman	6	Do
" " "	Geo. Slaughter	7	Thos. Slaughter
" " "	Jas. Wheeler	9	James Wheeler
" " "	Henry Glennister	9	Thos. Glennister
" " "	Edwd Glennister	7	Do
" " "	Fredk Glennister	6	Do
April 16. "	Willm Bignold	6	Willm Bignold
" 17. "	John Godfrey	6	Willm Godfrey
" 25 "	George Cripps	7	Isaac Cripps
" 30 "	James Taylor	7	William Taylor
June 4. "	Willm Plater	7	Joseph Plater
July 23. "	John Plater	9	Richard Plater

Part of a page from the Register of Leavers' Details 1844. Boys were admitted to the Lower School on the understanding that they had reading ability. When this was proved not to be the

RESIDENCES.	CALLING.	Dates and Reasons of Boys leaving the School.
Silver Lane	Bricklayer	July 19. 1852. Constant work.
Bull's Head yard	Labourer	Mar. 27. 1852. Expelled for non attendance
Whitehall St.	Shoemaker	Having obtained work. Nov. 17. 1851.
Church yard	Do.	May 26. 1852. constant work.
Castle St.	Sawyer	Obtained situation. May 19. 1853.
Walton	Shoemaker	May 24. 1852. constant work.
Parson's fee	Bricklayer	constant work. Feb. 5. 1855.
Bierton Road	Labourer	in attendance. October 18. 1851.
Cambridge St.	Do.	Expelled by order of the Trustees for irregularity
White hill	Policeman	Feb. 29. 1852. expelled for non attendance.
Do.	Do.	Dec. 18. 1852. Obtained work.
W. Bull's Head	Labourer	in attendance. October 18. 1851. Expelled by order of the Trustees for irregularity
Do.	Do.	Oct. 25. 1852. irregular attendance
Castle St.	Registrar of births &c	irregularity in attendance. Dec. 13. 1851. Expelled by order of the Trustees for
Do.	Policeman	irregular attendance. June 14. 1853.
Silver lane	Carpenter	July 28. 1853. constant work.
Whitehall St.	Labourer	Oct. 25. 1852. irregular attendance
Do.	Do.	
Back St.	Carpenter	Oct. 18. 1853. irregular attendance
Do.	Do.	
Cambridge St.	Maltster	larity of attendance. Dec. 13. 1851. expelled by order of the Trustees for irregu-
Walton St.	Baker	obtained situation. Feb. 24. 1853.
Workhouse yard	Labourer	march 23. 1854. constant work.
Do.	Do.	Oct. 25. 1852. irregular attendance
Do.	Do.	march 30. 1854. constant work
Bierton Road	Do.	Mar. 11. 1852. expelled for non attendance
Silver St.	Cabinet maker	
Whitehall St.	Carpenter	Dec. 18. 1852. irregular attendance.
Bierton Road	Labourer	Oct. 25. 1852. irregular attendance
Back St.	Do.	
Market Square	Nickmaker	

case, they were required to withdraw. Withdrawals under this heading disappeared in the 1860s.

Dates of Admission.	NAMES OF BOYS.	Ages of Boys.	NAMES OF PARENTS OR GUARDIANS.
May 8th	Hugh Pratt	15	Annie Pratt
" "	Samuel Holden	13.6	Henry John Holden
" 9	(E.) Ralph Sidney Johnstone	9.1	Henry Christopher Johnstone
" 15	Tom Rolls	12.9	Edmund Rolls
Sepr. 18	Christopher Roads	12.6	Francis Roads
" "	Henry Pierre Lucas	12.5	John Pierre Lucas
" "	John Cooper Lucas	10.1	" "
" "	Alfred Lucas	8.1	" "
" "	Charles Ernest Curtis	13.5	Robert Curtis
" "	Douglas Harold Griffin	8.5	Harold Griffin
" "	(E.) Charles Miles	12.10	George Miles
" "	(E.) Chs. Wm. Ivatts	12.6	John Charles Ivatts
1900 Jan. 22	Thomas Henry Field	13.11	Edwin Field
" "	Fred Edward James Smith	9.9	William Smith
" "	Snow Harry Turnham	11.11	Henry Turnham
" "	Henry Thomas Turnham	10.3	" "
" "	Percy Ferdinand Turnham	8.9	" "
" "	Arthur Lane Elliston	9.10	Robert Joseph Elliston
March 5th	(E.) Fredk. John Robinson	13.	Alexander Robinson
" "	(E.) Charles Stanley	13.3	William Stanley
May 7	John Hall	13.5	William John Hall
" "	Leslie Edward Jenns	9.8	Fredk. William Jenns
" "	Edmund Leslie Rolls	7.11	Fredk. Charles Rolls
June 12	Frank Percival Lander	8.11	George Lander
Sepr. 17	Jack Grist	11.3	John Wesley Grist
"	(E.) Cyril John Wheeler	9.9	Frederick John Wheeler
"	(E.) John Eschman Jarvis	9.3	Valentine Harry Jarvis
1901 Jany. 21	Horace William Hunt	14.9	George T. Hunt (Uncle)
"	William Butcher Hughes	14.9	John Beecham Hughes
"	William John Tweddle	9.	George Tweddle
"	William Thomas Bell	10.2	Thomas Bell

Part of a page from the Admissions Register 1900. The names include a number familiar in Aylesbury during the ensuing years. Robert Locke had a son who continued his coal business

RESIDENCES.	CALLING.	Dates and Reasons of Boys leaving the School.
Marsworth	Widow (of Farmer)	Jan. 21st 1901 – to enter a Bank.
Ayl. & N. Marston.	Tailor	Sep. 16 : 1901 : To business.
22 Tring Rd	Accountant (Pr. Wks)	Mds. '06 – in Bank
Weedon	Grocer &c.	Sep. 16 : 1901 going to business
Upton, Dinton	Farmer	Sep. 16 : 1901 to a boarding school
Walton St.	Pawn-broker	Jan. 21: 1901 To Business (with father)
"	"	June 1902 Left the Town
"	"	" " "
Lower Hogshaw	Farmer	May. 13\1901. To business)
Grove farm, Bierton	Farmer	Mids. 1907 – Business
Stoke Road	Gardener	Sep. 16 1901 To work
Kingsbury	Shoe-maker	Sep. 16 1901 To work.
Stone	Engineer	May 13: 1901 Boy Clerk H.M.S.
7 Market St.	Butcher	Mids. 1904 – Away to School
Waddesdon	Hotel-keeper	Jan 19th 1903 To Bedford County School.
"	" "	Easter 1905 – business
"	"	Xmas '05 – Business
Tring Road	manager of Printing Works	March 16. 03 Going to Berkhamsted
16 Granville St	G. W. Station Master	Jan. 20: 1902 Clerk on G. W. Railway.
35 Walton St.	Cycle-maker	Apr. 1902 To business (with father)
Aston Clinton	Farmer	May 13th 1901 With father.
Kingsbury	Furniture-dealer	Mids. 1903 away to school
Weedon	Wesleyan Minister	Jan. 20. 1902 left Weedon (for Staffordsh:)
Waddesdon	Hotel. keeper	Jan. 19 1903 To Mag. Coll. Sch. Brackley.
Bierton	Commercial Traveller	Mids. 1903 " " " "
13 Albert St.	Foreman at Milk Fac.	Mids. 1904 – Business
47 High St.	Draper	Mids. 1907
10 Church St	missionary in China (deceased)	Mids. 1902 Business
Hogshaw	Farmer	May 5. 1902 With father.
Bambridge St	Draper	Private S.
Bierton	Farmer	Mids. 1905 – Withdrawn

in Buckingham Street, became a governor of the Mixed School and Mayor of Aylesbury.

of the Trustees – Lord Carrington. As the Member of Parliament for Aylesbury, then living at 'The Lillies', Weedon, Lord Nugent was also in a position to have access to it.

A letter (the report ?) in the Trustees' archives (CH3/13/10) noted 'the large, lofty, well ventilated' room in which the examination took place, but immediately complained of the poor discipline – 'much whispering and talking among the boys.' It was clear that 'the system of instruction ought to undergo a thorough change … it is merely mechanical and cannot develop the faculties of the boys.' The record of the townsmen who were present (which was included in a *Brief* to the High Court of Chancery) was much more damning (CH3/L1/16). It referred specifically to 'books below the degree of attainment boys should have reached at their age … great ignorance of the most primary rudiments of the Latin language … all were very ignorant of the church catechism and Scripture history.' They were equally 'ignorant of the compound rules of arithmetic.' Many 'could scarcely read'. In fact their attainment was 'far below the attainments of scholars in the National and British Schools' … (closer) to that of 'village day schools in bygone days.' Reasons given by the staff were that the boys were 'idle, had no capacity to learn and were irregular in their attendance.'

A 26-page document, signed by Rev. John Pretyman, Vicar of Aylesbury and Edward Green, merchant of Brook Cottage was sent to the Lord High Chancellor. His Lordship ordered that 'all parties concerned do attend him on the petition,' which was dated 26 August, 1850.

The *Brief*, as it was described, began with a review of the history of the Charity, its provisions for 120 boys and the financial situation. The first complaint was that no information concerning the Charity had been made public since 1832. The blame was put upon the trustees, none of whom came from Aylesbury. It was pointed out that 'Every inhabitant of Aylesbury and Walton has a vested right in the benefit of the Free Grammar School,' but that there was no representative among its trustees. Many other issues were raised, but it was considered that they could be best dealt with in a comprehensive *Brief* setting forth precise proposals. A single marginal comment written by someone in the Lord Chancellor's office anticipated at least one reaction to the future *Brief* – 'There are strong reasons why the residents of Aylesbury should not be trustees … with the exception of the clergy, there are few if any suffi-ciently qualified by education to superintend the conduct of the school and the chief tradesmen of the town are so connected in business that they would be open to suspicion.'

The report upon the case submitted to the Lord High Chancellor when published, concluded that:

'The trustees of this school appear to me to have neglected their duty, and to have altogether omitted to carry into execution the Decree of the Court of Chancery of 1720, which they were bound to do. The circumstances, however, of this case are such, arising in a great measure from the length of time which has elapsed since the Decree was made, and from the powers given to the Court by the statute of 3rd and 4th Vic., c. 77, that it is in my opinion impracticable to produce the reform required by any attempt to carry into effect the Decree of 1720; but that they may be obtained by the Order of the Court of Chancery, and that therefore it is nec-essary that a fresh application should be made to the Court of Chancery. The existence of the Decree of 1720 will not prevent this course from being taken. The best course for this purpose is to present a Petition under the 52nd Geo. III, c. 101, and under the 2rd and 4th Vic., c. 77, for a scheme to regulate the Charity, and to introduce the changes which are required by the present state of society. This petition should be served on the trustees, and before the Master (under the order to be made) the various points in dis-pute will be settled, in the presence of the Attorney-General. I have, therefore, refrained from expressing any opinion on the propriety of the various changes required to be introduced, and as to the persons proper to be appointed trustees, whether by virtue of any office they may hold, as the Vicar, or otherwise, as these matters will depend on the view taken by the Master in the Court when the facts are fully before him: the petition, however, should state fully the facts of the case and the alterations and amendments proposed to be introduced by the petitioners. The costs of this petition, both of petitioners and respondents, will be borne by the funds of the Charity. This course is the speediest and least expensive which can be adopted, and is that which I advise to be adopted on behalf of the inhabitants interested in these schools. (Signed), JOHN ROMILY – Lincoln's Inn

The second document from the petitioners to the Court of Chancery bore the title *The State of Facts and Charge* and was dated November 19, 1850 (CH3/L1/2). It was essentially a scheme for a board of management. It began with a series of complaints regarding the management of the Charity. It repeated the charge that no information had been made public since 1832. The homes of the trustees were listed. None was in the immediate vicinity of the town. The nearest was six miles from Aylesbury (Oving). Others were Whaddon Hall (22 miles), Wilton (16 miles), High Wycombe (15 miles), Lattimer (14 miles), Amersham (10 miles), Chesham (12 miles) and Winchendon (10 miles). It was suggested that trustees should be resident within five miles of the school house, that they should have four meetings annually, and that the names of new trustees should be posted at the doors of all churches and chapels and near the door of the school. Furthermore, 'if any Poor Rate payer has any objection to any of them, he should report it and propose another.'

The finances of the school called for particular attention. Within ten days of December 1, a copy of the accounts should be available for public inspection by the ratepayers of Aylesbury for one week daily between 10.00 a.m. and noon. A banker should be the treasurer of the Charity and a fire-proof chest, spring-locked with two keys should be purchased. Among other items there should be placed in it the plans of the estates and properties of the Charity. No one should be employed for profit under the Charity. In June and December, advertisements should be placed in two Aylesbury papers and two London dailies about the school. The Charity should also support an exhibition available for three years worth £50 a year to be held at an English university. (Unknowingly, this recalled a proposal for a similar exhibition for Oxford made in 1790 (CH/3/E3)). It was recommended that the age of entry to the school should be seven and that the qualification should be an ability to read. The statutes of the school were also required to be printed.

The comments contained in the *Observations* of the *Brief* emanating from White, Eyre and White of Bedford Row were limited, but explicit. Of the

		William Jeffrey Graham
✓ 1887	U. 1	Forest Outlaws
		William Turvey
1893	U.1	Life of Wellington
1894	II G.C.	A Book of Golden Deeds. C. M. Yonge
1895	III. 2	Smiles' Boys' Voyage
1897	IV 1	Bible
		Ingram Plested
1887	U. 1	Half hours in the Far West
		William Cowley
1893	G. L.	Kingston's Arctic Adventures
		Harold Percy Cowley
1887	U. 1	Half hours in the Far East
1888	U. II	Life of Nelson
		Percy Landon
1893	U. 1	Robinson Crusoe
1894	II 2	Robert Dick . Smiles.
1895	III. 1	John's British Birds.
✓ 1896	IV. G.C.	Darwin's Naturalist's Voyage.

A page from the Prize Book 1860-1924.

school staff, it was suggested 'it would be beneficial to get rid of them.' As for the proposals concerning local trustees, it was felt that they would be likely to make election 'a source of jobbing' while 'busybodies and do-nothings' could allow themselves to be nominated by 'the mobocracy of Aylesbury'. The trustees had always 'been selected from gentlemen of all political opinions totally unconnected with the town so as to be free from influence in a place where political feeling is very strong'. As for the printing of the statutes, that was regarded as 'a useless expense'.

As a result of the submission to the High Court, a new 'schedule' was put into effect. Fourteen trustees, all living within ten miles of Aylesbury, wth the Vicar of Aylesbury as chairman, were nominated. Five trustees constituted a quorum. A banker was to be appointed treasurer and the strong box was to be kept by him. Finally, the costs of the Court of Chancery were to be paid out of the school income.

At a meeting of the trustees (18/10/1852), with Lord Carrington in the chair, the new scheme was put into effect – and 300 copies of the statutes were printed by J.H. Marshall of Temple Street. Perhaps Lord Carrington had had enough. The expenses of the trustees for 1852 listed an item 'Journey to the Lord Carrington to sign a formal refusal to act as a trustee any longer.' At least he might have found comfort – more correctly cold comfort – in an article in *The Aylesbury News* (15/12/1849) which put the situation in a broader perspective. 'This is not the only charity in the country that has gone wrong ... in fact there is not a charity in England which is not abused.'

The staff of the school reported its own actions in response to the examination of the school. Mr. Heyward produced a new timetable and plan of instruction – not least for the 'hours of homework'. The Headmaster's response was to request more 'grammar books' ('The Eton Grammar' was favoured) and reading books ('with instructive extracts'). Mr. Cox also set in motion an inspired plan for the rearrangement of the desks in the large main school room – he upon a platform at one end: another teacher upon a platform at the other end, with the desks of the boys ranged around the walls and an empty space in the middle.

Henceforth the Headmaster's report to the meetings of the trustees was required to produce an increasing range of information. Besides applications for admission, departure of scholars and absenteeism (Philologius Ridley's irregular attendance called for particular attention 30/12/1860), medical certificates were being sought and complaints about punishments were required.

On the retirement of the Rev. Frederick Cox ('the bad state of the headmaster's house' a recurrent topic), advertisements were placed in six journals and yielded 32 applications. They came from Clerks in Holy Orders at Marlborough College, Lancaster Grammar School and Armagh College as well as from headmasters in a number of other schools. They were clearly unaware of the state of the school and its premises. The Rev. Thomas Gwynne was appointed (2/3/1857) but he moved to Andover Grammar School three years later. No reason was given in the trustees' minutes. The new advertisement was for candidates in Holy Orders 'with an M.A. from Oxford, Cambridge, London or Durham.' It was stated that there was a 'good house' and that boarders might be admitted 'on the Headmaster's own account'. The Rev. Alfred Howell of Christ's Hospital filled the vacancy.

Changes in the organisation of the school increased from the 1860s onwards. A scheme to divide the institution into an English school and a Latin school was initiated (10/11/1860). Several staff changes took place among the assistant masters, whose salaries appear to have been about £135 p.a. Mr. Ridley followed Mr. Crasler in asking for a salary increase (16/5/1864). The trustees replied that they must first 'consider the state of the funds.' Nor were they very enthusiastic about the proposal for monitorial assistance (22/3/1864). Presumably, there was a positive response to a request by a parent 'that the boys in the upper school should wear caps.'

In 1862, a new scheme for the management of the school, which must have pleased the townsfolk of Aylesbury, but not have surprised the trustees, was received from the High Court on behalf of the Charity Commissioners. It was entitled 'A scheme for the management of the Aylesbury Free and Endowed Schools', dated 15 July, 1862 and is quoted in full as *Appendix B*.

In brief, the scheme required the trustees to meet four times a year at stipulated times on the school premises. The audited accounts of the Charity were to be published in two Aylesbury newspapers two weeks ahead of the annual meeting. The staff was to consist of the Headmaster, the Writing Master and at least a second master who was to be called the Master of the Lower School. Boys were to be admitted at the age of seven and were required to be able to read. Those receiving 'gratuitous education' upon the Foundation were limited to 120. The syllabus in the Lower School comprised English Language, writing, arithmetic, bookkeeping, accounts, geography and modern history. The 'course of education in the Upper School' comprised Greek, Latin and French languages, mathematics and 'other useful branches of education.' There was to be daily instruction in the Scriptures.

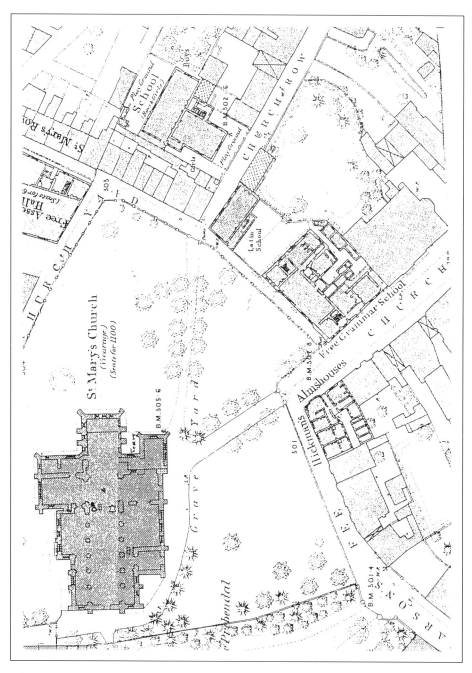

The site of the Old School in Church Street, formerly Broad Street (O.S. Aylesbury, XXVIII. 15/10/1885. Reproduced by permission of the Ordnance Survey).

Capitation fees were to be one and a half guineas per quarter for the Upper School and two guineas for boys residing outside the parishes of Aylesbury and Walton. At least ten 'exhibitions' were to be available for boys moving from the Lower to the Upper School. Boys in the Upper School were required to pay 2s/6d a quarter for the use of expensive books. The Headmaster was at liberty to receive twenty boarders to be instructed with the boys of the Upper School. The Headmaster and the Master of the Lower School were to live rent free in the school premises. There were regulations concerning holidays, discipline, the maintenance of attendance registers and the conduct of examinations.

The management of the school gradually improved. Admission and withdrawal registers were kept with greater care for both the Lower and Upper School. They not only listed addresses, which show a surprisingly wide catchment area, but also the 'callings' of the fathers. To cast an eye down the pages is to see distinct evidence of a bygone age. Groom and ostler, colporteur and cellarman, sawyer and cane chair maker, coach builder and whitesmith, hay merchant and grazier, watch maker and butler mingle with a variety of railway employees. The registers would prove a fruitful source for a local history study. A list of prize winners was started in 1862. Sometimes a leather-bound book (complete with the confusing inscription *Scol. Gram. Aylesburiensis 1620)* has been handed down through three generations of pupils who have attended the school. The titles of all the books and their prizewinners were recorded.

The conduct of the annual examinations, with experienced examiners appointed well ahead of the event and submitting their reports punctuallys also reflects a management change. No complaints were reported at the meetings of trustees. In 1885, the trustees called for the names of boys who had entered for the Oxford and Cambridge local examinations during the last five years. They advised the headmaster that 'as many boys as possible should be entered (henceforth) ... even at the risk of failure'. In June 1888, the Endowed School Prize Giving and the examiner's report were published for the first time. The prefatory remarks of the Chairman, Canon Evitt, centred upon the noble example of the Duke of Wellington – it being the week of the commemoration of the Battle of Waterloo. The 'young soldiers of literature' who were receiving the prizes given by Harding's Charity, were reminded that 'success proves nothing, but honest labour does'. That year the examiner was the Rev. Octavius Ogle M.A. He examined 32 boys in the Upper School and 98 in the Lower School. The *viva voce* results were 'not very good' – perhaps, he conjectured, because the boys were 'questioned by an unknown examiner in an unfamiliar voice.' However, nothing untoward was registered about the 'examination of the slates.' Order and discipline were pronounced 'very good'. Copybooks were free 'from blots and erasures.' There was a 'commendable absence of litter' in and around the premises.

New staff were arriving. The Rev. Christopher Ridley became headmaster in 1893. Thomas Osborne (of 59 Grove Road, East Hackney) was appointed to the Lower School (salary £100 p.a. with accommodation). Miss Ridley was thanked for teaching drawing 'gratuitously'. The Rev. Christopher Ridley retired in 1903 and Thomas Osborne was appointed as a temporary replacement. From 1891 onwards, there looked down from the wall a copy of the Tower of London portrait of Sir Henry Lee, (where did the Rev. F.G. Lee discover the original which was only purchased by the Tower in 1989?).

Looking back over the nineteenth century, it is difficult to explain the general stagnation that the school suffered. In more general terms, it was partly because it was closely allied to the Anglican establishment in an increasingly strong non-conformist community. Possibly it was related to the division between the Free School and the Latin School, though the boys in the latter were so limited numerically that it could not have had any significant consequence. When it was the only school in the town, there was sufficient pressure upon it that many parents registered their boys for admission well before – in some cases long before – the time of entry at the age of six. And when boys came to the head of the queue, all too many lacked the required ability to read and were accordingly soon dismissed. Even more had to leave to take work because of the poverty of their families. In all such cases little benefit was derived from the school days.

A GREENFIELD SITE

The inadequacies of the school were crowding in upon the trustees increasingly as the century advanced. Already in 1869, the need for a playground was causing anxiety. The alternative was 'a site for the school premises to which a playground might be attached.' An approach was made to Harding's Charity (23/8/1869) to enquire if its trustees 'would be willing to co-operate with the trustees of the school' to discuss 'the educational needs of the neighbourhood'. Some £5,000 might be required. Harding's trustees were not prepared to provide more than £2,000. The local press was invited to give some publicity to the matter. The following year it was noted that 'Land situate in Bicester Road near the turnpike gate' was available at £150 per acre (7/5/1870). Shortly afterwards, Harding's trustees advised that there was land on the Wendover Road owned by Hickman's and Harding's Charities, as well as on the Bierton Road owned by Lord Carrington (16/5/1870). There, for the time being, the matter rested.

All the time, the old buildings of the school were deteriorating. There are references to the state of the roof, the floors, the water closets, the ventilation, the headmaster's kitchen. A surveyor was called in for a major inspection (15/12/1876).

The matter of a new school site was taken up again by the Charity Commissioners in 1885. It was suggested that what was needed was 'a good day school in which boys of the middle class whose parents are unable to send them to more distant boarding schools may receive such an education as will best suit them for the business of life.' The commissioners and the trustees agreed that the charity arrangements were capable of improvement. There were suggestions that fees from four to six pounds annually might be charged, with provision for the reception of boarders and scholarships for poorer boys on grounds of merit from public elementary schools of the district. A letter from the assistant commissioners (reported 18/6/1885) indicated that 'the provision of new buildings is indispensable and as long as the school is attached to the present confined site it is not likely that a satisfactory reorganisation can

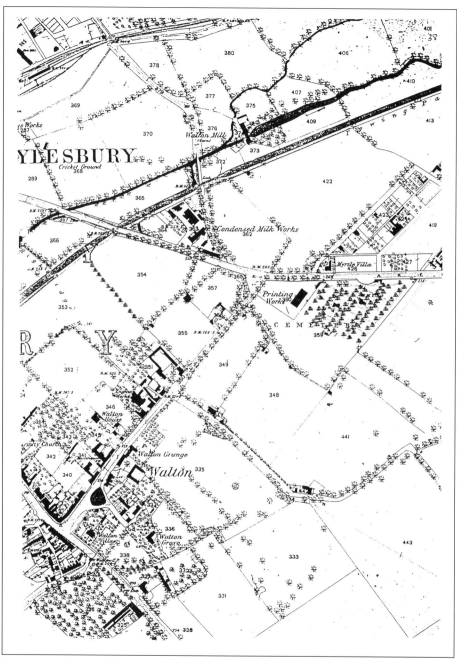

The site of the new Mixed School in Walton Road, fields 348 and 349 (O.S. Aylesbury 28/6/1880. Reproduced by permission of the Ordnance Survey).

Memorandum of **Agreement**

made the *first* day of *November* one thousand nine hundred and four **Between** The Right Honorable Nathaniel Mayer Lord Rothschild of Tring Park Tring in the county of Hertford of the one part and **Frederick Barford Parrott** of Aylesbury in the county of Buckingham solicitor the clerk to the Governors of the Grammar School in the parish of Aylesbury aforesaid as Agent for and on behalf of the said Governors (hereinafter called "the purchasers) of the other part.

1. The said Lord Rothschild (hereinafter called "the "Vendor") agrees to sell and the purchasers agree to purchase for the purposes of a school and school-house proposed to be erected thereon and the premises and playground in connection therewith the hereditaments described in the schedule hereto and the inheritance thereof in fee simple subject to the existing tenancy thereof and to all easements (if any) affecting the same at the price of One thousand four hundred and six pounds fifteen shillings to be paid on completion of the purchase.

2. The purchase shall be completed on or before the twenty fourth day of December next at the office of Messieurs Horwood & James the Vendor's Solicitors and the purchasers shall from that day be entitled to the receipt of the rents and profits of the said premises all outgoings up to that day being cleared by the Vendor. If the purchase shall not be completed on or before the twenty fourth day of December next the purchasers shall pay to the Vendor interest on the purchase money after the rate of Four pounds per cent per annum from that day until the completion of the purchase.

3. The title shall commence as to a part of the said hereditaments with a deed of partition dated the seventeenth day of February one thousand eight hundred and eighty and made between the Vendor of the first part Alfred Charles de Rothschild of the second part Leopold de Rothschild of the third

Memorandum of Agreement on the transfer of land in Walton Road from Lord Rothschild to the solicitor's clerk on behalf of the school governors, November 1, 1904.

be effected ... The trustees should ascertain whether assistance may not be looked for from ... some of the surplus funds in the non-educational charities with which the town of Aylesbury abounds.' It was observed that 'The bulk of the income from Harding's Charity is now applied to the payment of the apprenticeship fees of boys and girls.' The charities were to be invited to consider making some provision 'for the higher education of girls ... in connection with the Grammar School.' A special meeting was eventually convened in 1893 at which Harding's Charity promised a substantial sum and Bedford's Charity the equivalent of £250 a year (the sum usually given to 'paving the town').

'Lithographic' copies of a letter were sent to the local charities and a committee of seven, including three members of the school staff was set up in the name of Aylesbury Grammar School. Little progress was made. Hickman's Charity pointed out that its purpose was devoted exclusively to the provision of almshouses. And while the nearby Prebendal came up for sale in 1886, its site was not regarded as suitable for consideration.

By now, fifteen years had passed since the Education Act of 1870 which had been followed by the Acts of 1876 and 1880 that made universal elementary education compulsory. Financial provision from the local rates became easier under the Local Government Act of 1888.

The absence of games facilities was taken seriously from 1893 onwards – the mystique of team games having spread from the public schools. A cricket ground was rented for £8 during the summer months from a Mr. Gomme (9/10/1894) and a football field for £5 p.a. in Bierton Road (30/12/1894). 'The Town of Aylesbury' expressed dissatisfaction (24/8/1895) that there was still no financial prospect of going ahead with the scheme for new school buildings. But at least there was a crumb of comfort at the county level when in the summer of 1896 'the County Cricket ground' was made available for the pupils of the school.

Signs of a breakthrough came at the turn of the century. The fees now stood at £6 p.a. for boys from the town: £7 for outsiders. *The Bucks Advertiser and Aylesbury News* (5/10/1901) devoted 3½ columns to a rather desultory debate about raising a rate to pay for improved secondary education – an act taken by all of the counties adjoining Buckinghamshire. In 1902, the Balfour Education Act laid the foundations for the country's secondary education. The County Councils were thereby permitted to raise monies for secondary education from local rates. The Buckinghamshire County Council's scheme for secondary education and its implications were debated (28/2/1902), not least as to whether 'the foundation of a mixed school (was) an indispensible condition.' Further meetings were held later in the year. On July 2, 1903, by order of the Board of Education 'a new scheme under the name of Aylesbury Grammar School' came into existence.

Meanwhile the daily life of the school had to continue, with the shortage of space causing increasing problems for rather more than a hundred boys. A house in Church Street was offered to the trustees for £2,200, but declined: the possible acquisition of Ceeley House was discussed (22/6/1903). Inevitably, moving the school to a new site affected the use

Boys in the garden of the old school, 1904.

and value of the existing premises. There was uncertainty as to whether they could be sold to help raise money for the new school (24/9/1902). But at least a committee came into being (3/11/1903) to enquire into the purchase of a site.

The upshot was a letter sent by the trustees' solicitors Horwood and James to Lord Rothschild of Tring to enquire whether he would be 'willing to part with from six to eight acres of two fields adjoining Turnfurlong and Walton Road occupied by a Mr. W. Hazell or the field similarly occupied in the Wendover road adjoining the *Three Pigeons* and if so what price he would require for the same'. There was a positive response. Lord Rothschild 'was willing to sell 7¾ acres of land adjoining Turnfurlong Lane at £170 an acre as a site for the new school subject to the erection and maintenance of fences'. Two grass fields were thus acquired, following an inspection by a representative of the Board of Education. The Ordnance Survey map of 1885 was inspected and the area found to be 8 acres, 1 rood and 4 poles (12/7/1904). The agreement to purchase was dated November 1, 1904. The purchase price was £1,406/10/-. Walter Hazell agreed to give up the tenancy without compensation on the understanding that 44 poles adjacent to the Printing Works, described as 'mostly brook', were relinquished in his favour. They were acquired for the sum of £200. The signatures of Lord Rothschild and Mr. Hazell were incorporated in the handsome deed.

The Buckinghamshire County Council immediately offered a grant of £2,000 and, although the feasibility of a mortgage was debated, it was not immediately approved. Nevertheless, planning proceeded apace. The Board of Education gave approval for the appointment of an architect to draw up plans for a school for a hundred pupils, to be increased eventually to accommodate 150. At the same time, the clerk to the trustees made an application to the Chancery Division of the High Court of Justice for an order transferring the Personal Estate into the name of the Official Trustee of Charitable Funds. It was reported (15/1/1905) that 'an order' had been secured from the Charity Commission vesting the real property belonging to the governors in the official Trustee of Charity Land. The Board also stated that it had no objection to 'the alienation of any property belonging to the trustees to raise funds for the cost of new buildings and the purchase of land.'

BUILDING THE NEW SCHOOL

The Board of Governors (14/3/1905) agreed to invite competitive designs for 'a new mixed secondary school and a headmaster's house … to accommodate 75 boys and 75 girls as day scholars, planned with a view to convenient extension and one storey preferred'. Two playgrounds were required, with closets for the boys apart from the main building. Cycle sheds were also needed. The cost of the School was to be £6,000 (i.e. £40 per scholar): the headmaster's house £1,500. An additional £250 was to be set aside for laying out the frontage and for fencing.

Designs had to be submitted anonymously. From among them that bearing the *motto* (as it was called) *Kudos* was chosen unanimously. The architect behind *Kudos* was Mr. Claude Pemberton Leach of 21 Pelham Crescent, Kensington. All of the architectural plans had been available for public inspection and Mr. Pemberton Leach was sent copies of the also favoured other *mottos Bucks*, *Lustre*, *Light* and *Air*. An Aylesbury architect, Mr. Fred Taylor, was appointed to convert the design into a final architectural plan, bearing in mind the considerable slope of the site. Nineteen tenders were received, averaging about £7,500 in their estimates. The tender of Messrs. Hackersley of Wellingborough was accepted.

The school's modest investments were sold and a loan was arranged with Lloyd's Bank at 4% for thirty years. The well on the school side was considered 'quite insufficient' for the school's needs, so that water had to be laid on. Insurance had to be arranged. And one of the new governors had the happy idea of restoring the pictures of Sir Henry Lee and Henry Phillips. In fact, it is the first reference to a Phillips portrait (and the inscription on it was found to be incorrect). Mr. Izzard, the picture framer and restorer of Temple Street, appears to have undertaken the restoration. The governors also agreed that a 'tablet', painted and gilded and bearing the following inscription should be placed on the new school.

'Aylesbury Grammar School. These grounds were purchased and these buildings erected in the year 1906. The school was transferred at Easter 1907 from the old buildings in St. Mary's Square where it had carried on since its foundation in 1611.'

No one has been able to find this tablet or to account for the origin of the information in the second sentence. Certainly, no Old Aylesburian who was at the school in the 1920s remembers seeing it.

The furnishing of the school proceeded apace – hot water radiators to be fitted, furniture to be supplied from High Wycombe, fire precaution equipment to be put in place (handpumps, leather and galvanised buckets). Tennis courts had to be laid out for the girls. An extended list of science equipment was presented. The cricket pitch for the boys refused to respond satisfactorily to the new roller and mowing machine. The new groundsman was faced with the problem of levelling the turf. The Headmaster proposed the installation of a 'system of speaking tubes'. Instead, the governors proposed 'a telephone … if it becomes a necessity.' Ironmongery (from Jowetts), a tea urn (from Bradfords), three clocks (from Dukes'), a piano (from Whitackers), chairs (from Jenns') a shed (from Eaton's) – and the hire of a pony and cart (from J. Nappin) were among the trivia that were listed in the governors' minutes. Some 200 books came from the old premises – one 'from as far back as 1611'. Dr. Baker paid for some of them to be repaired. 'Proper paper' had to be bought for the water closets. The old school globe had to be covered with an up-to-date map. It was a nice touch that from the school windows and playgrounds Mr. Hazell's sheep could be seen on the grass keep that the school leased to him until it was required for other purposes. (Sir Henry Lee also kept sheep in the Vale – thousands of them according to legend).

By 1907 Mr. Osborne was in possession of the Master's degree from Oxford that was required of him (is it apocryphal that he cycled to Oxford to keep the necessary terms?). Mr. J.R. Smith a B.Sc of London (1906) was established as his right-hand man. Staff could now be recruited – Miss Kelly, Miss Foreman, Miss White, Mr. C.D. Cranmere and Mr. T.M. Foss. The salary of the headmaster was £350 plus the house. The total bill for the rest was initially £850. Fees were agreed at £7/10/- a term. The syllabus was to be expanded to include vocal music, drill, domestic economy and the laws of health. Sgt. Major Unwin was appointed drill instructor at five shillings and six pence a week and an old boy took on the post of the first laboratory assistant.

The *Adminissions Register* had a new format, including a space for future employment. The first admissions included fourteen girls. Among the boys were Thomas Osborne's son Ralph and his companion Brian Gadesden (who was to have a colourful career in Australia and Canada and whose son became Lord Mayor of London). It is worthy of note that out of the first fifty names listed under 'Employment' in the *Admissions Register*, twenty-one entered the teaching profession. This appears to have been independent of the fact that a pupil teacher centre established in Aylesbury in 1904, was transferred to the school in 1907.

Among those who became a pupil teacher was Alfred Young. His *School Journal* from 1907 gives some idea of the day-to-day programme of the ten boys that constituted his class.

The first governors consisted of four from the Buckinghamshire County Council, four from the Urban District Council, nine co-opted members and one from the Hebdominal Council of the University of Oxford. They agreed readily that representatives from *The Bucks Herald* and *The Bucks Advertiser* should attend their meetings. They also expressed a wish that staff should not smoke on the premises. At their meeting on February 1, they had proposed that 'Lord Rothschild should be invited to open the new school during the second week of May'. He telegrammed his acceptance. The ceremony took place at 3 o'clock on May 23.

In retrospect it can be appreciated how fundamental the introduction of state secondary education was for the school. Continuity of the Grammar School Foundation had been put at risk. Henceforth, the school was to operate on a totally different basis and to have a totally different character.

There was a footnote to the change. The buildings in St. Mary's Square were being put up for sale in two lots (CH3/E7). The sale was in the hands of the auctioneers and estate agents Messrs. Reader & Son, who had advised the school of their charges. These not only included news-paper advertisements and posters, but also the cost of 'Town criers in Aylesbury and at the Market and other towns in the district 7s/6d'. Lot One consisted of the Headmaster's house and the Grammar School (reserve £870). Lot Two consisted of the Second Master's house and the Latin School (reserve £880). They were described as 'fine examples of early eighteenth century brickwork with some choice examples of craft work in lead'. Before the auction was set in motion, Mr. John Reader gave an address, remarking how unusual it was to have ladies present on such an occasion. He imparted that he had personal associations with the building that he was about to sell. It was his own *alma mater.* There followed an extended talk on the history of the school before the bidding was opened. Lot One was bought by the Architectural and Archaeological Society for the purpose of housing a museum. Lot Two was acquired by the Vicar and Churchwardens of St. Mary's.

THE LEGACY OF THE OLD SCHOOL

It must be admitted that to employ the word 'legacy' in respect of the contribution made by the Old School is difficult. There was little in the way of tradition to hand over. There was not even enough money to provide a 'meat tea on the occasion of King Edward's coronation'. The boys must have left with relief the mediaeval centre of Aylesbury for the greenfield site in 'the other parish' of Walton. Some of the pupils who became the next generation of Aylesbury business men recalled the school with a measure of affection. Dr. George Locke and his three brothers all attended the school in the 1860s. Dr. Locke was decorated with the Order of Commander of St. John of Jerusalem. Thomas Field, seventh generation owner of the Market Square silversmith's shop, speaking at the dinner of the Old Aylesburians Association in February 1909, declared that he was proud to acknowledge that he owed his success in life to the education that he had received at the school. Contrastingly, Michael Hurd, the biographer of William Rutland Boughton (Oxford 1993) sketched a depressing picture of the composer's schooldays. 'Little was offered and little accepted. The elderly clergyman who functioned as headmaster carried out his duties more often than not in a doze from which his assistant was too tactful to wake him – his very owlishness endorsed by his name, the Rev. Mr. Howell' (p. 4). Rutland Boughton never displayed any attachment to his old school, though he received class prizes in 1889, 1890 and 1892. At a later stage he was treated proudly by the school's music master and actually composed the setting for the school song. C.C. Stokes, writing in *The Aylesburian* sixty years on,

Thomas Osborne M.A. Oxon, Headmaster, 1907-1927.

recalled 'the fear and trepidation' with which he had entered the school. He remembered a Hulcott boy riding to school on his horse and two brothers driving from Waddesdon in a pony and trap. Boys who did not have pedal cycles went to the playing field on the rear wheel step or cross bar of a friend's machine. As a choir boy at St. Mary's Church, he had to take time off from school when the service was held for the visiting Assize Judge. The winter of 1906 left a powerful impression with its never-to-be-forgotten snowball battles, with the boys of 'the British School' in Pebble Lane and those of the Church School in Oxford Road.

A contemporary of C.C. Stokes, Ernest Hunt, would appear to have been the first old boy to achieve the status of Archdeacon – albeit of Matabeleland and Bechuanaland. Thomas Baldwin, later editor of *The Bucks Free Press* left the school at the time of the transference to Walton Road to become a cub reporter at fifteen shillings a week.

Some of the old grammar schools in other parts of the country developed lasting traditions. The school premises in St. Mary's Square can have done little to foster in those who left them a sense of nostalgia, though the buildings must be seen in the context of their time. The staff probably had little time outside their teaching to practise what is now called pastoralism, a powerful force which attaches the young to an institution. Some of the blame for a lack of tradition must attach to the trustees. They consisted of men of considerable consequence who were certainly in a position to offer or to encourage others to offer endowments. And the unfortunate image of the school resulting from the findings of Aylesbury's radical petitioners lingered. Not many souvenirs of the Old School were carried to the new. The contents of the record box appear to have been divided eventually between the lawyer's office of Messrs. Horwood and James and the County Record Office. There should have been some valuable old books, but only the Reverend Mr. Howell's school Bible remains.

Nor did the school's property in the Manor of Broughton greatly help. As often as not, expenditure upon it almost swallowed up income. In retrospect, it is ironical that the Phillips' bequest was invested in the one area in the vicinity of Aylesbury where no significant suburban development was to take place. Supposing it had been possible to acquire land on the way to Quarrendon? But that leads to other speculations. Supposing that Sir Henry Lee had never left Quarrendon (for what was to become Ditchley) and that his mansion surrounded by sheepwalks had continued to grace the floodplain of the River Thame. It is correct that the name Ditchley should have been engraved on the succession of school plaques. Nevertheless, it was the descendants of a collateral of Sir Henry who, in the early eighteenth century, built the magnificent Palladian villa for which Ditchley is celebrated today. Meanwhile, Quarrendon where Sir Henry's heart lay metaphorically – and, indeed, physically, as well as the school that he founded were forgotten by the family.

Part 2

THE MIXED SCHOOL

'THE BEGINNING OF THE NEW'

At a meeting of the governors held in "the new schools" on Friday May 3 1907, the recommendations of the committee appointed to arrange a programme 'for the opening of the new schools' were approved. The governors had previously agreed unanimously 'to present Lord Rothschild with a silver key mounted with the Aylesbury Arms.' A pattern had been supplied by Messrs. Field and Son, whose family had kept a silversmith's shop in the town since the early eighteenth century.

Some four hundred attended the opening ceremony including the clergy of all denominations. The speeches of the Chairman and Lord Rothschild rivalled each other in length and were not without a difference of opinion. The Rev. Constantine Phipps began by congratulating the authorities and the architect on the splendid building. He remarked upon the 'handsome and picturesque' appearance of the school ... 'heated by hot water in addition to the fresh air stoves.' He intimated that he was not personally in favour of co-education and of children of different sexes sitting in the same classroom. Such things did not happen at 'Eton, Harrow or Winchester'. Nevertheless, changes were taking place. Lord Rothschild was more relaxed about mixed schools, referring to the favourable report of the Education Adviser to the London County Council where there were 122 co-educational institutions. He was not unaware of the differences between the attributes of boys and girls – 'boys have a greater power of conservative thought, while girls have much the greater power of expression.' He also believed that certain subjects were better taught by men than by women, in particular, mathematics.

The Headmaster proclaimed 'The end of the old order and the beginning of the new' and declared that his aim in the school was for 'one

THE PROGRAMME

Thursday, 23 May, 1907 at 3.00 p.m.

LORD ROTHSCHILD

will unlock the door and enter the school with the governors

SPEECH

by the Rev. C.O. Phipps, Chairman of the governors

LORD ROTHSCHILD'S SPEECH

Part song - 'Hunting Chorus from Rosamunde' - Schubert

THE HEADMASTER'S SPEECH

SPEECH BY MR. THOMAS MOSLEY

Chairman of the County Council

SPEECH BY MR. W.C. WHEELER

Chairman of the Urban District council

Part Song 'The Storm' - Hullak

VOTE OF THANKS TO LORD ROTHSCHILD

Proposed by the Rev. C.W. Pearson, Vice-chairman of the governors

Seconded by Colonel T. Horwood, Governor & Supported by Mr. F. Taylor the Architect

LORD ROTHSCHILD'S REPLY

Song - Now let us make the Welkin ring - Hatton

VOTE OF THANKS TO THE CHAIRMAN

Proposed by Mr. R.W. Locke, Governor

Seconded by Mr. F. Wilkins

THE CHAIRMAN'S REPLY

THE NATIONAL ANTHEM

class, one classroom, one teacher.' The Vice Chairman spoke of visiting similarly mixed schools in Normandy and hoped that in the future there might be links between the Grammar School and schools in other countries. The theme of the Senior Governor was 'The unmixed blessing of the mixed school' and his seconder anticipated the time when Aylesbury Grammar School would become the leading secondary school in the County. *The Bucks Herald* in its issue of the following Saturday concluded that 'the long-wished for educational ladder was now firmly planted.'

There was a sequel to Lord Rothschild's visit. In the autumn he donated shrubs for the front of the school and provided a second instalment together with trees the next year. The example having been set, the Duchess of Bedford followed suit, while gifts of seeds came from Messrs. Carter and Suttons. These gifts were not unrelated to plans to establish a botanical garden (3/1/1908).

The committee of governors grew in strength. Most of its members were recruited from a group of much interested and respected townsfolk, some of whose ancestors had lived in Aylesbury for generations. Local lawyers and doctors were co-opted. Local councillors sat beside representatives from the County Council. A rota of school visitors, including governors, was drawn up – quite independently of the inspectorate. And evidently all had every confidence in the new headmaster.

Thomas Osborne was given a free hand in recruiting staff. Apart from J.R. Smith, most of the staff that joined the new secondary school moved to senior positions in other schools. The Headmaster had an eye for academic quality as well as personality and experience. Ernest Jenkins (B.A. Trinity College Dublin) joined the staff to teach geography and music in 1910. The recruitment of a French assistant was approved – 'provided one of the Protestant religion can be found.' She came from Douai, stayed a year and was a great success. When Miss Foreman was appointed headmistress in Truro, the Headmaster travelled the rounds of the country to interview candidates whose applications he believed to be the strongest. He returned with Miss Jackson. Admittedly, there was plenty of choice with forty or fifty applicants for each vacancy. Lilian Waite, who had a London degree in French and had lived for two years in France, was appointed modern languages mistress in 1913. Miss Taffs with a Bedford College Froebel qualification, replaced Miss Haddon in

The staff and pupils in the first year of the Mixed School, 1907. The Headmaster, Thomas Osborne also produced the first 'panoramic' photograph of the school in 1920.

the same year. The recruits soon became a team whose members worked closely and affably together.

If ideas did not come from him, Thomas Osborne was not slow in picking them up from others and pushing them forward. They were stated succinctly in his monthly report to the governors and invariably approved on the nod. A prefect system was introduced. Apparatus was required immediately for the chemistry laboratory (6/10/1908): it was critical for potential matriculation and intermediate science students. Gymnasitc equipment came next (7/5/1909) – horizontal bars, climbing ropes, ladders, mattresses. Five pounds per annum was requested for a library of reference books – and rather more for a glass-fronted bookcase to house them. Where to teach woodwork was the next problem. It could not be conveniently undertaken in any of the existing classrooms. A temporary solution was found in premises in Kingsbury (2/7/1909). A cookery class was arranged (2/12/1909), but it was not until two years later that 'a good serviceable building' for £150 was erected for 'Domestic Science'. Miss Kay Davies came from Tewkesbury to extemporise with classes until such time as the building was suitably equipped. Naturally, domestic science had an urgent need for a sewing machine – yet another expense. A suggestion was received that an agricultural bias should be given to the curriculum, but it was not enthusiastically received. A request from the Drawing Master for stuffed birds and mounted butterflies met with the reply that he should 'write to Tring'. In the event, a collection of stuffed and mounted birds arrived independently from a donor some months later.

There was pressure from parents for a cadet corps. A minimum of thirty boys was needed to form a squad. Within a month, twenty had signed up and were 'willing to pay £1/10/- for their uniforms'. A rifle range was established. Rifles were promised from the Territorial Army but 'old carbines and rifles for drill purposes at 1s/6d each' were rapidly supplied directly from the War Office. J.R. Smith became the lieutenant in charge of the corps, with a second-hand uniform which was obtained for three pounds. The editor of *The Aylesburian* described him as being 'as much at home on the parade ground as in the classroom.' Route marches – the first seven miles in length – were regularly taken. A field day was held with the O.T.C. of Wycombe Royal Grammar School, with much successful 'skirmishing'. The cadets participated in the memorial service to King Edward VII with a much practised 'slow march' to St. Mary's Church. By 1914 the corps numbered forty. During the war, members of the corps stood by for action with their bicycles in case of air raids. They were mustered on six occasions. They also played a part in raising contributions for the War Loan, in the preparation of ration cards and in promoting the Coal Saving Movement. The cadet corps was disbanded in 1920.

The age of entry to the school, which had tended to be flexible, was fixed in 1908 at ten years. The numbers applying began to increase rapidly. The school opened in the autumn of 1907 with 103 pupils and six boarders. Among them was Alfred Young whose school journal from the Easter term of 1907 lists the weekly activities of his class (B.R.O./D/X 516). Surprisingly the timetable (9.00 a.m. to 4.45 p.m.) included four periods of Latin and of French. The marks obtained for all subjects were listed weekly: so, too, the number of times Alfred was absent or arrived late. At the end of each week the journal was signed by the master (J.R. Smith) and by the boy's father. The books used during the term were recorded at the beginning of the journal: the nightly homework, at the end. In 1909 Alfred Young took the matriculation examination after which he put away his tasselled cap (which now sits in a glass case in the County Museum).

The *Register of Admissions and Withdrawals* 1907-10 is an informative record of the pupils, listing their home addresses, the professions of their fathers and the school(s) that they had previously attended. The most distant residences were in Linslade from which presumably the boys came on 'The Cheddington Flyer'. In 1908, there were 138 pupils, including pupil teachers. Thirty-seven of the scholars had free places or County Council places or were Foundation pupils. For the rest, the fees in 1908 were £8/5/- annually or £2/15/- per term. A problem arose because the Board of Education stipulated that in County Council Secondary Schools a quarter of the places must be free. By 1912, there were 146 scholars and six pupil teachers. Technically, the school had exceeded the capacity of its accommodation. The numbers taking the Oxford School Examinations also rose steadily. Twenty-six passed the examinations in 1910 and three of them were sufficiently good to be exempt from matriculation. An honours board was erected to record the successes. Governors were invited to act as invigilators at examinations.

Increasing numbers were accompanied by increasing sporting activities and improved facilities were called for. In 1913, the governors gave permission for 'the erection of a pavilion by the scholars in the school playing fields.'

The Headmaster reported few difficulties to the governors. The paperwork arising from the examinations, the maintenance of records and registers took time. Occasionally the sum of five shillings was made available for secretarial assistance. Discipline seems to have caused few problems. Two parents removed their boys from the school and sent them to Berkhamsted because they found co-education unsatisfactory. Sixteen payments of school fees were outstanding in 1908, but numbers declined afterwards. The entire school body was insured against accidents for ten shillings a year. Only one injury seems to have been recorded in the first five years. There were occasional problems over the sons of small farmers who were needed at home for haymaking and harvesting. There was hardly any record of disciplinary action. In 1910, one of the half dozen pupil teachers was suspended for smoking and not wearing a school cap in the street.

From the outset, the Headmaster was interested in the progress of former pupils. He opened a register to record where boys had gone when they left school. November 1907 saw the first meeting of the Old Boys Association. The Association's programme included whist drives and social evenings as well as dances. In 1910 a holiday was proclaimed for Old Boys Day. In 1912, Thomas Burnham, who had won an open scholarship to Reading University College in 1909, was the first former pupil to graduate with an honours degree in science. Others followed him to Reading, Kings College London, and University College Southampton. The first old boy to leave a bequest to the school was Thomas Evans Denson. A prize for the most outstanding scholar of the year was established in his name.

The first Speech Day was held in 1909, the Old Boys' reunion being arranged to coincide with it. In 1910, the proposals were somewhat more ambitious, but neither Lord Roseberry nor Lady Battersea was able to accept an invitation, so the decision to hold the function in the Town

Hall was cancelled. In 1911, Lady Verney presented the prizes after which there was half an hour of singing by the pupils, a short (unspecified) Shakesperian performance and a gymnastic display in the open. The Coronation of George V was celebrated by a special holiday from June 19-24.

The Governing Body, which operated independently of the County Authority, sometimes found that it held different opinions. On the recommendation of the Headmaster it not only confirmed his appointments but also agreed the proposed salaries. As a result the salary structure of the staff was not free of anomalies. In 1910, the County Council recommended the introduction of a common scale of payment for staff employed in secondary schools throughout its area. The governors rejected the recommendation (6/5/1910). Later, they accepted a proposal that for the appointment of headmasters, the panel would consist of three governors and three members of the Higher Education sub-committee. The governors were also concerned about the withdrawal of scholars of poor families before they had completed 'their school life'.

It was natural that the Headmaster should become a member of the Future Career Association in 1910 and attend the Secondary Headteachers' Meeting organised by the County Council two years later. Meanwhile, Mr. Smith took charge of the evening classes which were being established. A prospectus of the school was printed and advertisements were placed annually in the local newspapers announcing the competitive examination for school scholarships. The number of these varied, but there were always four times as many candidates as there were scholarships. There were 56 candidates for twelve awards in 1914.

An unusual innovation was recorded in 1913. On behalf of the geography and physics classes, a request was put to the governors for the purchase of an apparatus for the 'recovery by wireless telegraphy' of reports about the weather. Within two months, Mr. Smith had the apparatus under control and messages were picked up from Paris and Germany. Hazell, Watson and Viney were also thanked for a gift of 'quite good telephones'. Exactly how they functioned is unknown, but they were described as being 'fitted to almost every room in the school.'

In October 1913, the Headmaster reported 'the time has come to consider adding to our accommodation.' Numbers stood at 158 and an increase was expected in 1914. But a shadow was soon cast over the plans. Even the existing accommodation was to remain available for only nine more months.

THE WAR YEARS AND AFTER

During the summer holidays of 1914, the governors were warned by Colonel Burrows of the local Territorial Army that in the event of hostilities the school premises would be required for a military hospital. Use of the 'wireless telegraphy' apparatus was banned after August 4. In October a requisition order from the War Office was received. A week's holiday was declared from October 16. The Minute Book (6/11/1914) recorded 'the school began work in its temporary buildings on Wednesday, October 28.' The accommodation consisted of two rooms at No.19 Kingsbury, two rooms in the Assembly Hall St. Mary's Square, two rooms in the Museum and one in the Church Hall. In 1916, the Victoria Club was taken over and the accommodation in the Museum and Assembly Hall vacated. St. Osyths provided a common room and accommodation for domestic science and woodwork. Cycles were housed in an outbuilding of The Prebendal. A formal agreement was signed with the War Office. Rent received from the military hospital paid for the miscellaneous facilities in the centre of the town. So, it was farewell to the greenfield site. The Headmaster declared the school to be 'fairly comfortably and conveniently housed'.

Thus began five difficult years. The governors held their meetings at St. Osyths, The Headmaster had to vacate his house for the medical staff of the hospital. The school playing field became something of a wilderness (there were no groundsmen available), the boys tried to maintain the cricket pitches. In order to keep the grass down, it was decided that the field should be let for grazing. A flock of sheep moved in. The deterioration of the site increased with a request from the War Office for the erection of huts to accommodate a hundred beds. Protests had to be made to the military authorities about the damage being done to the field. Lord Rothschild's shrubs were overgrown and neglected. In 1917, the botanical garden, now overgrown with weeds and site of a rabbit warren, was dug up for potatoes. Most of the sports field was subsequently ploughed up for the same purpose.

Staffing problems became increasingly acute. The Headmaster's right-hand man, J.R. Smith, left to join his regiment (his pay was made up to the teachers' level). It was fortunate that a replacement could be found in Mr. Morris, who was temporarily unfit for military service as a result of a breakdown through 'overstudy'. Soon, the four assistant masters were scheduled for enlistment. This presaged other problems. Was it possible for all of their salaries to be made up from the school's resources? Could their posts be kept open for them until after the cessation of hostilities? Would they have to agree to return before such a gesture could be made? In their absence, the posts were required to be filled by ladies (all of them temporary under the circumstances). To add to the problems, the domestic science mistress went off to an 'economy cooking' course and immediately afterwards left to join the Navy and Army Canteen Board.

In the minute Book of the Governors' meeting for February 9, 1916 (B.R.O. CH3/AM5) the sources of income for 1915 were as follows:

Board of Education Grants

Pupil teachers	£35
Pupils at £5 each	£500
25 pupils at £2 each	£50
Income from the endowment	£200
Income from school fees	£825
Other receipts	£70

Salaries amounted to £1723 and there was a record deficit of £380

By comparison with those arising from accommodation and staffing, other problems were minor. It was necessary to shorten the school day in early 1917 to fit in with the new railway timetables. In the same year, a number of farmers withdrew their boys from school to compensate for the loss of farm labour following conscription. The high cost of stationery taxed school finances and an additional half-crown was added to the fees. The autumn of 1918 was the nadir. The school had to close because of the epidemic of Spanish 'flu. Nearly half of the pupils were absent and the examinations had to be cancelled. Curiously, there was no reference to the Armistice in the Minute Book.

At the beginning of 1919, J.R. Smith and other masters began to return – Neaverson from the Land Army, Jenkins from the Navy. But still there was no sign of the release by the War Office of the school premises. In anticipation of the end of hostilities, the governors had written to the War Office about 'the desirability from a national standpoint of providing a military hospital at Halton in order that the school may be given back to the governors'. Major Lionel de Rothschild, the local Member of Parliament, was eventually asked to use his influence. By June, negotiations had reached the stage that a complete redecoration and reparation of the school was being sought. A week after schedule on September 30, 220 pupils were re-admitted to the school. In the interim, they had been promised a 'Peace Holiday', while the governors had been asked if they would like to apply for a German field gun as a trophy of victory. It was known as 'The cannon in residence.'

Recruitment to bring the staff up to strength now proceeded apace. A domestic science mistress (Miss Simmonds) arrived from Christ's Hospital, Hertford to be followed shortly afterwards by 'a drill mistress' (Miss Langham). Mr. Deeming was appointed after four years in the army. War bonuses were on the agenda of the governors and a School Teachers' Superannuation Act had to be discussed. 'Delapidations' (sic) at St. Osyths and at the Victoria Club had to be paid for. Provision had to be made for pupils who brought their lunches to school. Inflation disorganised budgeting. It was estimated that the cost per pupil had risen from £15 in 1913 to £24 in 1920. The entrance fee for examinations had also been advanced to £1/10/-.

In 1920, the annual ceremony of the Speech Day was restored. In 1921 because of the numbers attending, it had to be held in the Town Hall (rent £4). Attention was also turned to the sports field in anticipation of the restored Sports Days. A horse and mowing machine were hired from Mr. Nappin to cut the grass (£6/8/-). And the Old Boys Association returned to business. For its members the shadow of the war years lingered into the peace. A list of more than 200 Old Aylesburians who had served in the forces was printed in the magazine. One of their first acts was to open a subscription list to provide a 'stone tablet' bearing the

The main classroom of the Old School in Church Street as it was when converted into the principal display area of the museum c. 1920 (Courtesy of Buckinhamshire County Museum).

names of twenty-one former pupils who had died in the war. Names were inscribed on the memorial stone that was unveiled two years later. By then, the annual dance was attracting two hundred – more than enough to fill the school hall. The governors were also asked if the hall might be used for badminton, table tennis, draughts and cards. An Old Aylesburians tennis club was formed and used the school courts.

The demand for more accommodation, raised unsuccessfully on the eve of the war, became more vocal in 1921 and the school's architect, Mr. F. Taylor was invited to draw up plans for an extension. The County Council paid to bring army huts from Salisbury (at £75 each plus £30 for transport) in order to accommodate the workshop. The huts were occupied within six months of purchase (one was to serve as the woodwork room and subsequently as the art room until the early 1960s). More importantly, tenders were accepted for two new class-rooms (£456). The school was paying £25 a quarter for gas bills and these were calculated to rise as the facility was extended to the new premises. The 'advisability of installing electric light at the school' was debated (2/2/1923), but a decision was postponed for reasons of econ-omy. The proposal was turned down again a year later. But the County Authority produced the necessary £100 for the installation in the sum-mer of 1924. By the end of that year, the new biology building was on the agenda. At the end of 1925, a tender was accepted from a Waddesdon builder and, together with a locker room, the laboratory was opened two years later. In the meantime, a 23 year old biology master (Mr. Swallow) was appointed – to bring 'an infusion of young blood' into the system. He was also 'an enthusiastic scoutmaster' intent upon raising a school troop. (By this time, the school cadet corps had passed into history.)

Academic developments advanced steadily. In 1922, it was reported that there was a sixth form of twenty pupils – 'to which we have for many years looked forward.' The next year, one boy (unnamed) won a major scholarship in science, to be followed in 1924 by a girl repeating his success in arts. In 1926, the first 'major' scholarship to Oxford was achieved by Arnold Holland. A number of outside lecturers came to the school, one to talk about the League of Nations. An orchestra was invit-ed to give a concert to 'foster taste for good music' in contrast to the so-called 'comic productions.' A school visit, unique for its time, was planned to see the British Empire Exhibition at Wembley. Inspectors came and went, but no comments were recorded. They had no opportunity to observe how the frequency of the Headmaster's favourite hymns engendered irreverent mirth at the morning assembly – 'Soldiers of Christ arise', 'Fight the good fight', 'For all the saints'. Nor would they have appreciated the image of the Headmaster seen by the boys and girls – a cane held behind his back concealed beneath his gown. In 1925, the school was included in the County Scheme for the medical inspection of secondary schools. Two years later, an inspection was held.

Outside events occasionally impinged upon the school sufficiently to be reported to governors' meetings. In 1924, not least because the

The football team 1924-25, with Mr. Swallow in charge.

Improvements were made to the playing fields in the early 1930s. All hands were mustered for the operation.

catchment area of the school had extended to the margins of the Vale, fifty pupils were absent for several days because of a rail strike. The General Strike of 1926 had a similar effect. Two boys cycled fifteen miles from home each day to take their examinations. The Rotary Club offered to help pupils with such transport as its members could provide as well as with overnight accommodation. Mr. Cherry's 'Waddesdon Queen' stood by for action, but the Aston Clinton horse bus (used in inclement weather) was by now defunct.

A letter to the governors in the spring of 1927 from Thomas Osborne intimated his wish to retire while he was still active. It marked the end of the first phase in the history of the new school. The vacancy was advertised in *The Times Educational Supplement*, *The Journal of Education* and *Education*. The salary offered was £600 rising to £750, less £50 for the house and £20 for rates. 175 applications were received. Six candidates were short-listed. Three were graduates of Oxford; two of Cambridge and one of Liverpool. The youngest of them, an Oxford graduate, was appointed. George Pomeroy Furneaux came from the West Country where he already held the headship of Midsummer Norton County School. When he took over the school had 145 boys and 98 girls, with an established senior mistress in Miss V. Farmer and a vacancy to which he appointed C.G. Furley (thereby restoring Latin to the syllabus).

The new Headmaster took a number of initiatives within a year. Insurance was arranged for staff members (3s/9d per capita) in case of accidents to pupils in their charge on or off the premises. Provision was made for over seventy pupils, mostly from the surrounding Vale, to stay for lunch. Debating and philatelic societies, a chess club and a Savings Association were established. A fee of ten shillings a term was introduced for the use of textbooks while library acquisitions were published in *The Aylesburian* which came back into publication after several years in abeyance. The governors discontinued the representation of the press at their meetings. They presented a number of school trophies. The Christmas parties, held since before the war, were discontinued. The sports pavilion began to emerge from its foundations.

And, curiously, the Minute Books of the governors' meetings made no reference to 'The Housing Scheme' until 1928 when they recorded 'The Inter-House Cross-Country Run' and the summer sports day when

'Phillips House and Hazell (sic) House took the lead.' In fact, the House system was established in 1920. Four houses were suggested with the object of producing 'a Public School spirit of unity'. Six possible names were put forward – Denson, Lee, Hampden, Milton, Phillips and Ridley. Thomas Denson was the first president of the Old Boys' Association, the Rev. Christopher Ridley was the last headmaster of the old school. John Hampden was a logical choice. Lee (Sir Henry) had to wait until the 1970s. House masters and house captains were chosen, then the boys assembled in the playground, each house captain picking a boy in turn. The girls had an independent system of selection supervised by the then senior mistress Miss Violet Farmer.

A MEETING OF HISTORY AND MEMORY

In the story of the school the new régime marks a time when, for some readers, history and memory will come together. From the later 1920s onwards schooldays began to imply a six or even an eight year span. In 1928 the school was still a fairly intimate place. Classes were small. Everybody moved about in a much more limited space. The same faces were seen several times a day as they passed up and down the main corridor – the girls having arrived at the south entrance and the boys at the north. The majority of the staff stayed for a long time. The lines of discipline were clear cut and relaxed.

Outside the school the families of a larger percentage of the pupils knew each other or of each other. The town had a population of about 13,000 and the surrounding catchment area of the school probably had an equal number. Everybody met everybody in the streets, on social occasions, at places of worship (much more frequently than now), at the annual County Show and at places of entertainment. And, with the distinctively badged caps and hats, which all were required to wear, any new faces beneath them rapidly became familiar. Surnames were attached to the faces: sometimes nicknames – Chubby Jeffries, Squidger Parker, Smiler Grey, Pecker Betts – rarely Christian names. It was Fatty (Ronald) Aubrey, for obvious reasons. He became head chef at Buckingham Palace and published a book on the Queen Mother's favourite recipes. It was 'Cherry' Orchard, not least because of his rosy face. Where might his talents have led him had not his parachute failed to open during the early days of the Second World War?

The black-gowned staff, 'mortar board' in hand on formal occasions, appeared to grow shorter in the eyes of pupils as they advanced from Class One to the Sixth Form. Their idiosyncrasies, once the subject of mirth, became increasingly endearing. James Robins recalls the arrangement of cubes and cones set up for the drawing class and the heavily booted Mr. Buckingham intoning 'Perspective is the science of the true appearance of all common objects.' There were young recruits to the staff for whom girls confessed a secret infatuation: but there were no known 'Young Woodleys'. There were those who, like Harry Deeming, had a lifelong influence – a meeting of minds only to be explained by some mysterious personal chemistry.

In the early 1930s, the old Prebendal House (which the school trustees had declined to purchase forty years earlier) was standing empty and was bought by Miss Farmer, who gave up her post as senior mistress to provide accommodation for an independent school for girls and junior boys. She was succeeded by Miss Caldin who, in turn, left to become Headmistress of Carlyle Girls School in Chelsea.

A pillar of the institution retired in 1936. J.R. Smith, the indefatigable right-hand man of the headmaster, was a part of the school's living history. His gown had become threadbare after four decades of hard wear, but he remained as spry as ever. He was given a right royal retirement dinner at *The Bull's Head*. It pleased one of his younger colleagues that the 'old man' had lived to enjoy the 'halcyon days' in the life of the school.

A DECADE OF CONSOLIDATION

The foundations of the co-educational grammar school being fully laid, it entered a satisfying decade of consolidation. Oxford School Certificate Examination results averaged at least ten per cent better than those of the county at large. In almost every year a major county or state scholarship was awarded. For the girls, Joan Collier blazed the trail of state scholarships, went to St. Hilda's and obtained a first class degree in physics three years later. New honours boards had to be fitted into the limited wall space of the school hall, the winners of the annual *Victor Ludorum* ranking equal with the academically honoured.

Between 1929 and 1939 an annual account was given in *The Aylesburian* for each of the sporting activities. A list of all sports day results also appeared. Societies and clubs multiplied – debating, philatelic, chess, sketching, physics, biology. The Savings Association went from strength to strength. A School Needs Fund was established and a Barnado's Club. *The Aylesburian* also contained a list of new library books acquired annually. The captains of Phillips, Denson, Hampden and Ridley houses, each flaunting its chosen colours, were allotted space for their annual reports.

The range of sporting activities was extended, with the prowess of several masters the subject of legends. Lapses in discipline were rare. Two may be recalled. Although the entire male body of the school was expected to take part in the annual cross-country run, one year bred a resistance movement. All of its members started off boldly, but not far from the start a substantial number turned and sped home. The second lapse occurred on a sports day. It was not recorded in *The Aylesburian*, the pages of which it might have enlivened. The event was described by Maurice Severn in a letter sent to Mary Adams. He had been asked by the girls to show them how to adopt the running stride in hurdling – skimming over the hurdles instead of employing the old run-stop-jump technique.

'Unfortunately', he recalled, 'the loose canes on the posts which constituted the hurdles of the day were swept off by the trailing hems of the gym tunics and the experiment had to be abandoned ... Nevertheless come Event 33 on Sports Day, and before the starter and the steward could do anything about it, off came the tunics on to the pavilion rails and a bevy of contestants (with upper garments tucked into lower garments) presented itself on the starting line ... The pistol was fired. Not a cane fell, the spectators cheered and a new record was in the making. Alas, at the finish it was chaos. The timekeeper forgot to press his stop watch in shocked disbelief. The judge took his eye off the finishing tape which was dropped by his partner who averted her gaze. Nobody knew who had won. Much out of breath a senior mistress

The company assembled for the opening of the pavilion in 1930. A number of prospective Aylesbury 'worthies' are identifiable in the crowd.

rushed with an armful of tunics to redeem the situation.' Thereafter competitors in the high jump were allowed to wear white blouses and navy blue bloomers.

It was also Maurice Severn who was the first to take teams of boys skating when the floods froze in the Vale. Skating for girls was discouraged.

Despite all of the enthusiasm, athletic and sporting activities continued to suffer from the condition of the playing field. No headmaster could have worked harder to improve it. 'Plantains cover every square foot', he wrote in his first report to the governors. Rumours were rife that every boy would be expected to remove twenty-five a day. A lively groundsman was appointed at 55s/- a week and provided with the latest model motor mower with a seat above the roller. It was much admired, but was useless for any purpose other than cutting grass. A handyman was employed 'to level the outlying parts of the field.' Eighty pounds of grass seed were generously donated by Mr. Loader. But 4,000 square yards of ridge-and-furrow still required attention. When a set of new classrooms was constructed in 1931, the soil from the foundations provided the means of levelling at least part of the remainder of the field. More than ninety tons of earth were reported to have been shifted in the process. 'Practically every boy in the school has taken part', the headmaster reported to the governors. Some of the boys already had experience in moving earth, when the foundations for the pavilion were dug in 1929. The saga of the playing field came to an end in 1938 with the laying of tile drains (by the boys, of course) in the wetter area. Crumbs of comfort were derived from the trickle of water that drained from the pipes into the ditch the following winter as well as from the fact that in the final stages of the exercise, fragments of Roman pottery were unearthed. The new pavilion was ready for opening by Mr. Ralph Hazell on the occasion of the Sports Day in 1930. A new cricket pitch had been prepared (the school's own chain link measure employed for the occasion) and the untidy hedges around the field had been professionally laid. A concrete wicket for practice was available the next year. To the seven hundred pounds that had been raised for the erection of the pavilion, the governors added a contribution to cover the cost of installing electricity and water.

There was vain talk about the possibility of a school swimming pool in 1934, but a seasonal arrangement for pupils to use the facilities of the new municipal open air pool in the Vale had to suffice – facilities 'from June 1 to July 29, four guineas.'

Meanwhile, musical life in the school began to flourish. In 1931, Mr. Jenkins (The Christian names of masters and mistresses were rarely used) was succeeded by Mr. Pope, who was chosen from 253 applicants. The governors were asked to provide a new piano, Mr. Jenkins having used his own. A grand piano was acquired for the sum of twenty guineas. The next year, for the first time, a choir was entered for the Berks, Bucks and Oxon Music Festival. It came away with the Cecilia Cup. And it succeeded in retaining it for a second year. No less a critic

AYLESBURY GRAMMAR SCHOOL SONG

Words by
ANDREW WILLIAM HURST

Music by
RUTLAND BOUGHTON

Quick and strong

VOICE

PIANO

1. We

sing the Chilterns beech tree dressed, And our green vale we sing   With
Tud - or towers are tum-bled down   And Lee with Hamp-den lies;   And
shall the fame of Aylesbury rise Thro' dis - tant slow de-cades,   Till

Copyright, 1938, by Rutland Boughton

CURWEN

The first page of the school song, composed by Rutland Boughton with words by A.W. Hurst. The song was sold for a shilling a copy.

than Sir Hugh Roberton of the Glasgow Orpheus Choir acclaimed their singing enthusiastically. C.A.G. Pope, a friend of Rutland Boughton, went on to make a lasting impact on musical life in Aylesbury. In 1933 a small school orchestra came into being under the direction of Miss Ingram. It was as though hidden talents were conjured up, for school instrumentalists (pianists apart) were rare creatures at the time. Few parental pockets were deep enough to invest in string or wind instruments and there were certainly no school funds for the purpose. Such activities must have come as light relief to boys who were not especially adept at using the tools in the woodwork class or girls who faced the sewing of a gusset to stick in their needlework books.

Performances by the dramatic society became the norm. Sometimes they were given for charitable purposes – for 'The Mayor's Fund for Distress in the Coalfields' in 1929. In 1935 a most impressive entertainment, in which no less than 185 members of the school participated, was given in aid of the Royal Buckinghamshire Hospital Extension Fund.

The flora and fauna around Aylesbury provided plenty of opportunities for budding naturalists. Whiteleaf was a favourite area for field trips – finishing with a real Buckinghamshire tea at *The Plough Inn*. The 1939 visit saw a party of lepidopterists going off to collect specimens of butterflies and moths, while the botanists competed for the prizes offered for those who collected the largest numbers of different wild flowers. The winners collected 120 and 117 respectively. A few years later bee orchids and birds' nest orchids were still common in the same area.

In the 1930s school excursions became more ambitious. Anyone, it seemed, could go to Paris, but it was much more exciting for nine boys and two masters to set off from Croydon to Cologne on 'an Imperial Airways Liner' in 1933. Douglas Andrew still has souvenirs from this "first continental trip by British schoolboys by air". Admittedly, four years earlier and following a visit to the school, the distinguished pilot Sir Alan Cobham had given free flights to three boys and a girl. School excursions could claim to be big business when 200 pupils visited Southampton Docks, looked over *S.S. Berengaria,* and took in Salisbury Cathedral and Stonehenge on the return journey. Even bigger, if not better, was the hiring of a special train – 'The Chocolate Express' – to take 270 pupils to Bourneville. The Ford Works at Dagenham welcomed 230

Aylesbury Grammar School.

SCHOOL DRESS.

Girls.   The School Dress for girls consists of a **black velour hat** (obtainable at Miss Harper's, Kingsbury Square), a **navy blue coat, navy serge tunic and knickers**, and a plain white or cream blouse.

During the summer term a **panama hat** is worn.

The tunic. Length above the knee should be one inch off the ground when kneeling. The yoke ($2\frac{1}{2}$ inches) should be cut square and should be $2\frac{1}{2}$ inches below neckband.

The tunic should have three box pleats back and front, with a navy braid girdle, and should fasten, if at all, under the arm.

Older girls may wear a navy serge skirt instead of tunic, except for gymnastics.

The blouse must be untrimmed and should have a small turned-down collar and straight cuffs.

The navy blue coat is the standard outdoor dress.

A navy blazer is worn for general use in summer, and as an extra wrap in School in winter.

Hair ribbons must be navy blue or black, and slides must be plain and not coloured.

No jewellery, except a plain brooch or a watch, may be worn in School.

A pair of **indoor shoes**, as well as a pair of rubber-soled gymnastic shoes (white canvas tops), are essential.

Boys.   **The School cap and tie** (stocked by W. Thrasher, 7, High Street) are to be worn out of doors on all occasions.

Indoor shoes—the "Cambridge" shoe with leather soles— are essential, as well as rubber-soled shoes with white canvas tops for gymnasium.

During the **summer term**, the dress includes **grey flannel trousers** and the School navy blue blazer.

For cricket, all boys must wear white or grey trousers, with ordinary cricket shirt.

For football, **navy blue trousers** and **"House" jersey** (to be obtained at the School), with a cricket shirt available in addition.

Dress regulations in the 1930s.

in 1938. The last of these mammoth events took place in 1939 when a visit was made to the locomotive works at Derby, to Players' cigarette factory and to Boots pharmaceuticals at Nottingham.

Between 1929 and 1939 numbers of pupils grew from 265 to 346. Inspectors were especially aware of the pressures and inadequacies of the school premises. There was 'an implicit need for a gymnasium', the school hall being unsuitable for what was called 'drill.' Boys and girls were supposed to have separate classes. The 'offices' had to be extended and a 'sanitised spray apparatus' was acquired. The physics laboratory was too small. More classrooms were eventually opened in 1931, but there were no formalities. It was considered that, in view of 'the national crisis', it would be in bad taste. Gas radiators had to be purchased to heat them. The school's hot water system, operated from an erratic boiler, stoked with coke by Mr. Beechey, was inadequate for the purpose. Coal fires in the staff rooms called for occasional visits from the chimney sweep, who was paid out of the headmaster's petty cash.

Although it was unlikely to provide any immediate accommodation, it was with considerable foresight that the governors acquired for £1,000 what was known as 'Hazell's Workshop Building' on Turnfurlong Lane. The lease to 'The Small Holdings Committee of the County Council' was due to expire and Mr. Hazell was prepared to accept the offer. About the same time, the District Council was pressing for the widening of Walton Road and seeking to acquire some of the school frontage. In due course a new pavement backed by a retaining wall and an oak fence appeared. Pressure upon accommodation also implied increasing reluctance to let the premises for evening and other classes.

During the decade, discipline raised few problems. Only once were boys accused of stealing and even then the case was dismissed by the local magistrate. The first expulsion of a girl took place in 1931. 'Miscreants tended to be the same regular few', one Old Aylesburian recalled. Some masters gave offenders an occasional tweak to the ear. With unerring aim, one master would toss a rubber at an inattentive pupil. Saturday morning detentions (later transferred to Friday afternoon) were recalled as occasions when endless columns of figures had to be added up, when laboratories had to be cleaned or footballs pumped up. Four detentions in a row called for a visit to a senior master and the likelihood of the cane. Some first year pupils wondered if they had fallen foul of a punishment when for reasons of nature study they were required to root out bindweed in the school garden. 'Follow it down for a foot or more and you will eventually get it out', was the advice to Robert Wilson in 1948 by Miss Taffs. Her 'epitaff' (as Donald Wheeler put it) might have been written in bindweed.

Annual medical checks had to be endured. The compulsory wearing of school uniforms in accordance with the instructions sent to parents, was regarded as a discipline in itself. Certain shops in town enjoyed the monopoly of supplying the required items. Caps caused less objection among the boys than panama hats among the girls. They especially objected to pulling a straw hat over wet hair when leaving the swimming bath.

Parents caused occasional problems. There were fairly frequent requests to remove children before they had reached the stipulated age of sixteen. Sometimes parents had to be chided because of their children's absences. Only rarely were there lapses in the payment of fees. If children suffered lengthy illnesses, it was not unusual to apply for a return of fees. There was no explanation when, in the early 1930s, it was decided that staff members must live within two miles of the school. The cycling prowess of the staff was the subject of a poem in *The Aylesburian*. Advice on careers, even about applications to universities which were at the time much more demanding in basic entry requirements, was rarely sought or given. Most of those who went on to tertiary education (as it is now defined) contemplated a teaching career. Indeed, the school supplied in the long term an entire cadre of teachers, headmasters, headmistresses and educational administrators.

The school had been unusually fortunate in the health of its staff; but in 1938, the first fatality had to be recorded. Palmer Brodie, an exceptionally popular young master, was killed in a car accident. His parents bequeathed a school trophy in his memory.

During the decade, the school governors and staff became increasingly conscious of their position in the town's educational structure as well as of the growing strength of both the local and national education authorities. Not surprisingly, there was some friction as a result of a press release about a proposal by the Education Committee which was likely to have a fundamental effect upon the character and status of the school. Without reference to the governors and staff, plans were published for a prospective new school in 'California' and for the conversion of Aylesbury Grammar School into a Technical College. The plans were shelved in the face of events of far greater consequence.

'SCHOOLING IN AN EMERGENCY'

In August, 1939, there was an exchange visit between a German School in Bremen and High Wycombe High School. Aylesbury Grammar School shared in the exchange with parents accommodating three of the Germans and two Aylesbury girls paying a return visit to Bremen. Here, they experienced the opening of the autumn term in the school playground 'to honour the flag and salute the Fuhrer'. On the entry of the teacher into the classroom, 'the girls rose to reply to her salute of 'Heil Hitler' '. The visitors obviously received the full treatment, attending a Labour Camp for German youth and a meeting of the *German Girls League*. They could scarcely have appreciated that such features were a part of the Nazi system that was leading to the outbreak of the Second World War. And what could have been the thoughts of members of the school hockey team that had enjoyed such a pleasant match with a boys' team from Dusseldorf in the same year?

On July 26, 1939, an air raid precautions document was received. Precisely a month later the staff was summoned back to town in order to make preparations for the immediate reception of Ealing County Boys School and Ealing County Girls School. Their pupils were among the large numbers of evacuated children – labels round necks, bags and cases in hand – who were crowding into the reception centre in the Town Hall. The staff might have received a document prepared by the Board of Education, but it was of limited assistance in dealing with the infinite variety of tasks required on the ground and at the drop of a hat. Above all, there was insufficient room to accommodate two additional schools in the Grammar School premises. As a result Ealing County Girls School was transferred to High Wycombe. A Cox-and-Box arrangement was made to accommodate the Aylesbury and Ealing schools. Aylesbury children used

A school cricket team in the late 1930s.

the premises in the mornings (including Saturdays): Ealing boys were taught in the afternoons, when the Grammar School used the sports field if it was possible. The Wesleyan Methodist Hall was soon leased by the Grammar School. Afternoon classes were held there and the school clubs and societies met there. While all these arrangements were being effected the Headmaster was inundated with letters asking for admission to the school for children who had been evacuated privately. It was eventually agreed that such boys as could be admitted would attend Ealing School classes while girls would join the Grammar School.

The schools settled down to their new lives without major incidents during the first year. If an air raid warning was sounded, children had to remain in school until the 'all clear'. Air raid shelters were built. A senior teacher was appointed 'gas identification officer'. The indispensible satchel now contained a gas mask. Mark Tapping recalls that he was among those from the school who volunteered to assemble gas masks at an empty shop in Buckingham Street.

Examinations proceeded as usual. It was encouraging that there was no deterioration in the results (indeed, they were declared the best ever in 1942). Donald Dormer distinguished himself and the school by coming first out of 2,500 candidates in the Open Competitive Examination for entry as an apprentice in the Royal Air Force. There was one embarrassing incident when a member of staff, a conscientious objector who had received 'unqualified exemption from all forms of national service', had to be asked to leave as a result of pressure from parents, staff and boys alike. The summer term continued until August 3 and there was a short vacation term before the reopening in September with 370 Grammar School pupils and 110 Ealing boys. It was then that the first direct taste of the war was experienced.

On September 25 a bomb was unloaded on to nearby Walton Grange. The effects of the blast on the school buildings was considerable – loose tiles, split door-frames, shattered windows, and cracked ceilings. The thirty items listed were speedily repaired. At least the Chairman of Governors, Canon F.J. Howard, was able to report the good news that the first old boy to be decorated, W/Cdr Pearce (1912-14), had been awarded the DSO and DFC. Attention was now turned rapidly to blacking-out the premises, the application of anti-splinter netting to the window glass and the preparation of sandbags. Summer time continued through the winter and was succeeded by double summer time. Air raid shelters were extended, but soon began to leak in the winter rains. Rotas for fire-fighting and fire-watching were compiled. It was rapidly discovered that it was impossible to operate inside the school roof because of its structure, but large quantities of fire resistant liquid were sprayed around. Personal accident insurance for boys had to be arranged. Sleeping facilities were organised for the fire-watchers – Mrs. Furneaux bringing cups of cocoa to the bedsides, as Dennis Davies recalls. Staff and pupils undertook duties together, a memorable camaraderie developing. 'Dragons' and disciplinarians became friends, Daphne Edgar recalls. An Air Training Corps, Flight 599, was established with Maurice Severn as its Commander. Twelve senior boys volunteered to act as despatch riders. Collections for various charities were replaced by contributions to 'Aylesbury War Weapons Effort'.

All senior boys and girls spent most of the summer holidays in 1941 in their own personal war effort. Work was undertaken on farms, in factories and for the War Agricultural Committee. There was a new concern about public health. More than 400 members of the two schools had dental examinations in July 1941, while 250 were given diphtheria immunisation. In the autumn terms, 270 pupils were reported as having morning milk. The rationing of clothing soon called for action on behalf of growing children. All pupils were weighed and measured annually for their special allocation of coupons. The length of the foot and the size of the shoe were also measured in 1944, by which time the school had a selection of gym shoes which could be borrowed for drill.

The local authority established a 'Rest Centre stores hut' behind the school buildings. It was piled high with beds and bedding – but had no heating. Heating for the school at large gave cause for alarm, the 1924 boiler becoming increasingly erratic in its behaviour. The school itself was scheduled to be a Rest Centre if and when required. Sad news came in 1941 of the first casualties among Old Aylesburians, but cheering news of a military cross for R.A. Farmer and a DFC for Ivor Oliver. Nor could it be forgotten that there were some Old Aylesburians in occupied Europe. Vera Burr, married to a Dutchman, spent the war years in Holland.

With memories behind them of an active musical year, an Anglo-Soviet Week, a day school on Russia at High Wycombe, collections for Warship Week, and a number of lectures on the state of the world, the summer vacation of 1942 was keenly awaited. Most of the Ealing boys had returned home and only a minority returned for the autumn term. Forty Grammar School pupils and eight masters went off to a farm camp at Steeple Claydon organised by Mr. Bartlett. They clocked up 3,000 working hours collectively, shocking, loading and casting grain or cutting down thistles. Forty others went independently to farms and fifty into factories. In the summer of 1943 the exercise was repeated, with fifty boys a week attending the camp and sleeping under canvas while thirty girls, billeted in the school, dealt with the catering and domestic chores.

Mary Mays recalls endless hours hoeing between rows of cabbages. Barbara Fell recalls receiving sixpence a day 'pocket money' and, together with other girls, picking rose hips (to make rose hip juice for babies). The camps were repeated in 1944 and 1945, the school holding the record for the most 'boy-hours' (including 'girl-hours') worked in the county. Having established a reputation in the Vale for its agricultural achievements, it was not surprising that a *cri de coeur* should come from Whitchurch in the autumn of 1944. A field of flax, too low for cutting, needed to be pulled by hand. The following Saturday, 78 pupils harvested seven back-breaking acres at £10 an acre.

The services of pupils were also required at Christmas time. The postmaster regularly asked for assistance. Forty senior boys responded to his

The teaching staff in the late 1940s. The Headmaster G.P. Furneaux and Mrs. Furneaux in the centre.

first request and it became a tradition well into the post-war years. The school visitors, who continued to operate by rota for the duration of hostilities, strongly supported all this activity. No comment was recorded from the visiting Board of Education officials.

Throughout the war years, societies and clubs continued as best they could. The Debating Society flourished, with plenty of heckling from the audience. The Annual Oratory Contest yielded some interesting topics. 'My experiences in the Black Market' was a product of the time. 'Experiments on animals' and 'Nursing as a career for men' anticipated the future. Who (it may be asked) drew from the hat 'The Channel Tunnel is not boring.'? And has he or she lived long enough to be able to experience the Tunnel itself?

There was a slow return to something approaching normal in school life after the Victory in Europe celebrations in 1945. Blast walls, sandbags and air raid shelters were removed. The threat to Mr. Cowdray's motor mower, for which there had been no petrol during the war, was lifted. The restoration of school meals came on to the agenda. The Rest Centre hut was bought for £35 and became one of the succession of temporary buildings that was to mark the school site for fully thirty years. The Old Aylesburians Association was revived and received permission to use the school premises as in the pre-war years. Communication was restored with former pupils who had been in occupied Europe. Careers talks became part of the curriculum, though two years' national service took care of most of the boys who left during the next decade. Senior staff could apply for posts of special responsibility. Life was lean, rationing was to continue for several years, and there was little or no capital for the maintenance of existing buildings let alone for the construction of new. And the school governors appointed their first lady chairman – Mrs. Paterson – to deal with the situation.

In the school year 1945-46, there were 475 pupils and the population of the school's catchment area had increased to 45,000. Already in 1943 there had been discussion in the district about the provision of new schools for the future. In 1944, the minutes of the governors' meeting referred to the prospect of 'a co-educational school for 600 on a new site.' At a later meeting (September 1, 1944) there was debate about building a new school on the playing fields and the provision of new sports facilities on Walton Grange fields. It seemed that the Mixed Grammar School, as it had come to be recognised and appreciated in the course of forty years, was likely to suffer more than strains and stresses before it attained its half century.

POST-WAR CHANGES

The school had barely begun to recover from its wartime experiences when the contents of the County Development Plan for schools was made public. Aylesbury was already undergoing rapid growth in housing and industry. The small county town was changing in shape and character – the more so as a result of the new housing estates built to cater for the overspill of London. In March 1947, the governors were presented with a plan which showed that the school was scheduled for closure in 1962. The response was a proposal, which was accepted, that the existing Foundation should be continued as a voluntary school for boys from eleven to eighteen.

In the immediate post-war years, school numbers settled down to 420 plus. They were taught by twenty members of staff (whose 'service books' had to be kept up to date and who earned a combined total of £810 a month in 1946). In that year, Peter Scheuer had the distinction of being elected to an Open Scholarship in Natural Science at St. John's College, Cambridge. The sixth form had already exceeded fifty in 1947. New ground was broken that year by Margaret Carter when she was awarded a Buckinghamshire Music Exhibition at the Royal Academy of Music as well as by the award of the first Ph.D to a former pupil. Record numbers were being entered for the School Certificate Examination, though there was dismay that the entry fee had increased from £1/7/6 to a massive £2/15/-.

Late in 1948, the governors received notice of the proposed new secondary school to be built on the Turnfurlong estate. Since the governors were not even provided with a rough sketch of the plans and had not discussed the future of the Grammar School itself, they were not in a position to give their views as requested to the Divisional Executive of the Education Department. In anticipation of the change, the governors received a letter from the District Valuer assessing the value of the school buildings and playing fields as between £35,000 and £40,000, plus £7,500 for the headmaster's house and garden.

At a special meeting, it was decided to leave financial considerations on one side and to concentrate on which options would be best for the school. Preference was for a mixed school with aided status. Failing that, a boys' grammar school would be favoured over a mixed school with controlled status. Discussions were held with Mr. J. Leonard, the Deputy Chief Education Officer (and formerly a senior member of the school staff), about the various merits of voluntary aided status and voluntary controlled status. Consideration also had to be given to the siting of the school. The options were twenty-five acres at Walton Grange, nineteen and a half acres of Sheffield's land in Turnfurlong and thirteen and a half acres in Janes's field in Wendover Way. It was expected that the proposed secondary school would be built on the Walton Grange site, consequently the governors considered that Janes's field could best accommodate the two new Grammar Schools. There was provision in the Development Plan for a voluntary aided boys' school and a voluntary controlled girls' school. This suggestion was preferred by the Education Authority, but the governors believed that if aided status for a boys' school was refused, then they would prefer a mixed voluntary school. No formal resolution was taken on the matter, but the Authority was advised of the preference.

Formal notice of approval of the Development Plan was received in a letter dated December 12, 1950 and the school was advised, that if an application for aided status was to be lodged, it would have to be received before June 6, 1951. In May 1951 application was made for aided status with a proviso to the Ministry that the application be direct-ed immediately to the period while the school remained in its present buildings. A meeting was arranged between representatives of the school and of the Ministry later in the year. The Governors, determined to do their best for the future of the school, explored all options. In fact, it was too late to opt for independence as had been the case with certain other schools in the county. The Governors wished to know, in the event of the school being controlled, what would be the future of the founda-tion, the buildings and of their own powers. By the end of the school year, the governors received from the Ministry, 'for their consideration', the standard Articles of Government for a Controlled School. By August 22, 1952, no longer willing to defer a decision, the Ministry made an Order and Aylesbury Grammar School became a controlled school.

While those deliberations were continuing a number of more immediate problems were taxing staff and governors alike – a falling intake, the preponderance of girls over boys, the composition of the sixth form and changes in the examination system.

By 1949, the school was reduced to a two-form entry. The Headmaster predicted a steady decline in numbers for the next three or four years, with an annual loss of 80-90 pupils and an intake of 60-70. In 1949, 52 children had passed the entrance examination of whom only twenty were boys. There were even three girls who had gained entry at thirteen. In the following year, of the 73 new entrants, 50 were girls. In the school at large, there were 26 more girls than boys, while in the sixth form there were 31 girls out of 64. In order to avoid the difficulties of imbalance in a co-educational school, the governors recommended to the LEA that in future thirty places be allocated to boys and thirty to girls. By 1950, a balance had been achieved in the first-year entry, though the problem continued among new entrants to the middle school.

At the top end of the school, there was a new situation among the pupils who had passed the Higher School Certificate with distinction, but who chose to remain at school for another year. They were discouraged from taking the examination a second time, but there appeared to be no alternative course. The question was urgent and inseparable from the availability of major county scholarships, none of which had been awarded despite outstanding results. Such, indeed, was the case in 1949, with sixteen pupils achieving Higher School Certificates, four winning State Scholarships, 56 passing the School Certificate and 30 qualifying for the London Matriculation. The governors were highly impressed and recommended an extra holiday as well as agreeing to make personal contributions towards the cost of prizes for the most outstanding boy and girl of the year.

While examination results were going from strength to strength, a shadow was cast by prospective changes in the examination system. The new certificate of education was scheduled to come into force in 1951, with the so called 'Ordinary Level' and 'Advanced Level' examinations replacing the existing School Certificate and Higher School Certificate. There were two major changes in the regulations to which both staff and pupils objected. The first was that pupils had to be sixteen years of age before they were allowed to sit the 'O' level examination. Secondly, matriculation which, hitherto, was obtained on the results of the School Certificate examination, could henceforth only be achieved by candidates passing at least two subjects at Advanced Level as well as in other subjects prescribed at Ordinary Level. Furthermore, only eighteen-year-old pupils would qualify for matriculation status – that is for university entrance. There were direct implications for the teaching programme. The sixth form work would have to be widened to accommodate pupils working for both 'O' and 'A' levels. More important was the effect on bright pupils who were prevented from proceeding to advanced work because of the 'O' level age restriction. In the first year that the new regulations came into force, thirteen pupils were immediately affected. It was not long before some pupils began to leave without proceeding to the university entrance qualification. The regulations generated considerable unease among the 21 members of the teaching staff. To cope with the additional sixth form work and examinations procedure, the case was made for additional staff.

These academic and organisational matters must be set in the context of the slowly improving material situation and day-to-day school life as it was experienced by the pupils. School heating was gradually improved, though coke supplies were still at a minimum even in the hard winter of 1946-47 when teachers (like other people) had to fetch their weekly coal ration from the railway yards in buckets. Electricity supplies were subject to regular disruption throughout 1947-48. The pressure of gas might be so low as to prevent the cooking of meals. And the provision of meals emerged as a primary matter beyond the teaching and sports programme.

In the days of Headmaster Osborne, a lunch time precedent was set when daily at 12.30 p.m. he would go to the kitchen, take on the role of a father figure and carve the joint that Mrs. Grover had cooked. Senior girls would carry meals across the tennis courts to the staff room to be served to the waiting teachers. The children who had paid their shilling for the meal would sit between Mr. Osborne at one end of the table and Mrs. Osborne at the other. Those children who had brought sandwiches would eat them in the hall after a prefect had said grace. Here, they sat on the coconut mats which were used in the gym classes.

In 1946, it was decided to try and reinstate midday lunches, refurbishing the old kitchen and dining room (which could also be used as a classroom). In this way, the Headmaster thought that seventy children could be accommodated in two sittings. Nevertheless he had the unenviable task of deciding arbitrarily who should be admitted to the school lunch because there was insufficient space for all who wished to eat. Following a visit to the canteen at Wolverton Grammar School, he reassessed the facilities and came to the conclusion that the equipment could meet the needs of a hundred pupils. Unfortunately, the number who now met his criteria for admission reached 125. The solution was to provide four hot meals a week for 125. With the addition of a new cooking stove, it was found that 180 could be fed for four days a week in two sittings. Before new challenges arose, an alternative solution to the midday meal was forthcoming.

Meals, of course, called for food permits – and additional permits for each increase in numbers. Pupils remember the wartime diet that continued into the post-war years. Meat was rationed. Tinned spam, corned beef and snoek offered alternatives. Soya bean sausages helped out: so, too, did occasional whale meat. Some sort of uniformly brown gravy covered boiled potatoes and seasonal vegetables. Egg powder and dried milk helped to provide puddings. Seasonal fruits might be available, but with sugar rationed they could not be sweetened. Saccharine soon cloyed. Syrup was a luxury. Somehow, British Restaurants contrived to be more imaginative than most school canteens. School staff were regular visitors to the British Restaurant in the Town Hall. Naturally, alcohol never appeared on the school premises. Tobacco fumes seeped out of at least three of the staff rooms.

The School Meals Sub-committee in the Education Department, more than aware of the pressures on the Grammar School, decided that the canteen should be closed in favour of a larger one on the Walton House site of the Technical School across the road. It solved the problem of feeding, but raised other irksome issues. The Grammar School had to supervise its pupils, collect the fees and plan the twice hourly movement of scores of children across Walton Road. There was friction over the provision – and removal – of a pedestrian crossing as well as over a dividing wall in the canteen to separate Grammar School and other diners. It was a sure sign that life was back to normal when the school was able to open its own tuck shop in the mid 1950s. Hundreds of pounds were raised for the School Needs Fund, though the problem of litter threatened its closure. Penny biscuits reached the record number of 24,000 in one year (the staff favoured threepenny digestive biscuits). It was not long before an aspiring mathematician calculated that, if all of the penny biscuits sold were laid end to end, they would reach from the school to Stoke Mandeville. 'The visit of the school dentist', a contribution to *The Aylesburian* may have been one consequence.

In the bleak atmosphere of the immediate post-war years, the contributions of a talented staff were clearly a source of inspiration. None was more exciting than the stimulus given to the musical life of the school by C.A.G. Pope. By now he was well into his stride. Before his time music in the school had been something of a hobby. Now it had a new status. He set about creating a proper school orchestra. Three instrumental classes – in violin, trumpet and recorder – were held every week.

The annual House Music Competition (which still flourishes) was introduced. School choirs entered county competitions. The lack of instruments and expertise did not curb the school's musical ambitions when in 1946 Gluck's *Orpheus* was performed at the school concert (which had opened with the performance of Rutland Boughton's school song). A piano, recorder and a string quartet constituted the orchestra. Talent was also nurtured and encouraged by the performance of such works as Purcell's *Dido and Aeneas* and a cantata for choir and orchestra set to Dryden's 'Arise ye more than dead' by a pupil Kenneth J. Plested. According to Plested, the school orchestra was now a reality, having violins, cellos, recorders, clarinets and trumpets. Next came Handel's oratorio *Alexander's Feast* by which time the range of lessons available for instrumentalists had expanded to include double bass, flute and cornet. Palestrina's *Stabet Mater* followed. And 'the man behind it all' (as Plested put it) was also the man who was simultaneously transforming music in the town. C.A.G. Pope founded Aylesbury Choral Society, the Aylesbury Orchestra and the Aylesbury Youth Orchestra, encouraging members of the school to participate in their activities and strengthening the school's orchestra as required by bringing in instrumentalists from the town. Members of the school's Music Society participated regularly in the large-scale choral productions under the baton of Mr. Pope for which the town became celebrated. Handel's *Messiah* was, needless to say, among the first. It was not long before the school aspired to present its own performance. It was through opportunities such as these that Maureen Plater, a soloist in school productions, became the first pupil to win a place at the opera school in London.

Mr. C.A.G. Pope's school orchestra rehearsing about 1951. Charles Pope was the most influential figure in the musical life of the town as well as of the school.

The productions of the Dramatic Society were no less ambitious. *She Stoops to Conquer* by Oliver Goldsmith kept the company on its toes. *Tobias and the Angel* was judged to be 'the best ever'. Even more enterprising were the French plays that were produced by C.G.S. Furley. The first were plays written in French by English authors for English audiences. *Les Deux Sourds* (The Two Deaf Men) by Jules Moinaux was much more demanding and was praised by the local paper as 'almost flawless'.

With hostilities over, it was pleasant to resume school trips and visits. Set books for the Higher School Certificate had provided an excellent excuse for a sixth form visit to *Julius Caesar* in the early 1930s. Now, it was *Hamlet* with Robert Helpman at the Memorial Theatre in Stratford-on-Avon, Donald Wolfit in *King Lear* at the Campden Theatre and *Antony and Cleopatra* with Vivien Leigh and Laurence Olivier. Perhaps such visits stimulated the school's first attempt to produce a Shakespearean play. The Dramatic Society graced the new school hall in 1954 with a full length production of *The Merchant of Venice*. In the same year a festival of the arts was inaugurated in Aylesbury. The junior section of the Dramatic Society won a second class certificate with excerpts from *The Taming of the Shrew*, while a first class certificate was awarded to the cast of a French play *L'Anglais tel qu'on le Parle*.

A Sixth Form excursion to Switzerland provided the experience of an abundance of sweets and chocolates (which were still strictly rationed at home). A visit to West Germany shortly afterwards revealed the heavy damage suffered by Cologne and Dusseldorf. (What had happened to the members of the boys' hockey team from Dusseldorf who had played a match at the school in 1938?) The Rhineland was revisited in 1964. Normandy was also on the agenda. The sights seen must have moved the boys in particular. Hampton Court, Blenheim Palace and St. Albans provided cultural entertainment. Technical interest was provided by Clarendon Abbey Nuclear Research Laboratory. Field excursions were made to both Devon and to Cornwall.

During the immediate post-war years, the school was to celebrate the 350th year of Henry Lee's endowment. The commemoration took place on February 17, 1949 when Canon Howard, a former chairman of governors, and The Rev. H.A. Byard, a prospective chairman, conducted the service. The academic staff went in procession from the parish hall (once a part of the old school) to St. Mary's Church (beside which the original classroom had stood). In addition to commemorating the endowment, the occasion also served to remember former pupils who had fallen during the 1939-45 war. Shortly before the commemoration on February 2, a memorial plaque had been unveiled in the school hall. It was dedicated to the twenty-nine boys and two girls who had lost their lives. The occasion was made the more significant by the presence of boys who were engaged in the two years' military service which was a requirement at the time. A commemoration service was held at St. Mary's on a number of occasions during the following years.

The Festival of Britain in 1951 also called for celebration. School parties paid visits to the London exhibitions, while the Dramatic Society made its own contribution to local festivities. An episode dealing with the foundation of the school was presented as part of a pageant held at The Prebendal. The visit of Queen Elizabeth to Sir Henry Lee at Quarrendon provided the excuse for an interlude during which the Queen was borne unsteadily on a litter by 'three stalwart youths' down a positively hazardous terrace. At the conclusion of this episode, with a considerable amount of poetic licence, the Queen charged her champion to found a school. Appropriate music, 'The Lady Oriana', was under the direction of Mr. Pope.

In the sporting calendar, traditional events continued. One year, the cross-country run might be through mud flood and rain (106 participants); the next over hard, dry ground that threatened to twist ankles (200 participants). One year, the swimming gala at the open air baths might be held in brilliant sunshine; the next, it was so cold that competitors had to wear coats between events. More important was the fact that considerable numbers of pupils began to obtain life saving certificates. The range of events at the annual Sports Day was increased, especially for the girls. Standards were increasing sufficiently for a team of four boys and a girl to represent Buckinghamshire at the Schools' Athletics Championships held in Bath. Subsequently, the school was represented at the All England Schools' Championships. The school having acquired a cine-projector, it was natural to produce a film of the athletic activities. After four months' work on processing and editing, the school's first film – five minutes long – was finally ready. It could hardly expect to produce the same response as a private viewing at the Aylesbury Odeon, of the fourteenth Olympic Games held in Switzerland, or as the film of the 1936 Olympics that inaugurated the School's Bell and Howell Gaumont apparatus. No film of the 1952 Olympics was shown. If it had been perhaps an old boy, F/O Eric Dafter, might have been seen as an Olympic torch bearer. Meanwhile a considerable reputation was being acquired by the women's hockey team, with Audrey Dunn the first to be selected (as centre forward) for the Bucks County Junior XI and Miss Haggerty as the Vice Captain of the Bucks Women's County Hockey Team.

Miss Haggerty was also responsible for another welcome innovation. In answer to complaints from the girls that the boys could not dance, she established a Dancing Club, with subscriptions at a shilling annually. With the purchase of dance records and an electric pick-up, the club was soon in full swing. Harry Davidson recordings provided polkas, two-steps, waltzes, Irish reels and quick-steps. Such was the demand that in a short time an amplifier and loudspeaker were required.

Among school societies, the Scientific Society took on a new lease of life. There were specimen hunting trips to the canal and Hartwell Pits. Smaller animals and insects were mounted. An aquarium was acquired. There were visits to such companies as the then thriving International Alloys, to the Aylesbury Gas Works and the Dunstable Meteorological Station.

The pupils were as involved as much as ever with work in the community. The branch of Dr. Barnado's was particularly strong. Out of Aylesbury's 500 members, the school had 200. It had its own protégées. Aylesbury cots were supported at High Close in Wokingham and, at Babies Castle at Hawkhurst, one mischievous infant was described as having curls all over his head and bright twinkling eyes (where is he today?). One boy was supported by the school to train as a bootmaker and another was helped at Watts Naval School. Demands on pupils' time and pockets was becoming so great that the governors decided to limit the number of flag days supported to six – the RNLI, Alexandra Rose Day, The Blind, St. John Red Cross, Poppy Day – and, of course, Barnardo's. But the choir more than compensated for any curtailment.

They raised money for the Friends of Europe Fund, Chilton House Old People's Home, The Lord Mayor of London's United Nations Appeal for the Children of Europe and Save the Children Fund.

The end of the decade witnessed the retirement of two stalwart members of staff. Miss Taffs, who had held generations of juniors in awe and had taught a miscellany of arts and crafts, retired after 37 years. Miss Langham was still the indefatigable teacher of physical training after 31 years of hyperactivity. Miss Stewart, the senior mistress, resigned on her appointment to a headship in Guernsey. The next year, G.P. Furneaux decided to retire after 24 years as headmaster. The School's halcyon days of the 1930s – despite the social and economic stresses at the national level – had been a rewarding time for him and his family. They had enjoyed the big rented school house. Three sons and a daughter had passed successfully through the school. During the war, all sorts of burdens and restrictions had been endured. Unfortunately, for a headmaster, the cessation of hostilities brought no immediate relief.

Sometimes the problems called for considerable diplomacy. Three instances may be given. First, when the so-called Iron Curtain descended upon Europe in 1948, Parliamentary debate on the role of Communists and Fascists who were working in the public service filtered down to the local level and were not without effect upon school governing bodies. There were known to be teachers at the school whose political affiliations fell into the category mentioned in the Commons. The local press raised the issue and certain town counsellors called for action. The Headmaster's opinion of the colleagues concerned was sought by the governors. Happily, he had little difficulty in convincing them of the integrity of his colleagues. They were committed teachers, good family men and would be unlikely to allow their political beliefs to interfere in any way with their work.

Secondly, there was an issue based upon manpower allocations. It emerged the following year when the Headmaster wanted to appoint two women teachers. He had to wait for a response from the Ministry of Education regarding the possible effects of the appointments upon the ambiguously titled 'Bucks Quota of Mistresses'. With backing from the governors, the appointments were made regardless of the quota. In retrospect it merits attention that these issues were handled directly by the Headmaster. Trade unions played no part, though a number of staff belonged to the essentially non-political Assistant Masters' Association.

In the third instance, there was a difference of opinion between the school and the Chief Education Officer and Schools' Management Sub-committee. The Head Postmaster sought the assistance of a number of senior boys to help with the Christmas mail, a request which was at variance with the policy of the CEO and the Committee. The governors, supporting the Headmaster, noted that they were not bound by the policy of the Education Authority and seemed to take some pleasure in asserting their independence.

THE PASSING OF THE MIXED SCHOOL

In January 1952, the newly appointed Headmaster took over from G.P. Furneaux the 'voluntary controlled' Grammar School with some 400 pupils. Lionel Tidmarsh had been selected from among eight short-listed candidates. He came from Lady Manners School – a mixed Grammar School – in Bakewell. From the outset he proved a popular choice. His staff meetings were conducted punctiliously and the careful preparation of their minutes is still recalled by his colleagues. Not least among the early innovations was the introduction of a system of special responsibility allowances.

In February 1953, the school was faced with an inspection for the first time in twenty years. At the time, all inspectors' reports were printed as special Ministry documents (H.M.S.O. S.G. 50.1953). The inspection by a small team of full-time Ministry inspectors seems to have been a very civilised proceeding. The report, written in a simple and effective style, paid much attention to the physical handicaps of the school premises. It underlined the lack of facilities for private study by the expanding sixth form (the Headmaster had intimated that there was at least a need for a prefects' room). The report acknowledged the problems of selection from among the large number of applicants drawn from at least 34 primary schools. It remarked upon the pronounced mobility of pupils coming from Wendover where there was a substantial number of R.A.F. families. All subjects were deemed to be satisfactory (with the 'intellectual

Lionel Tidmarsh (M.A. Oxon), Headmaster 1951-1967

contribution' made by geography teaching described as 'especially praiseworthy').

Nor did the Headmaster fail to impress upon the inspectorate his concern about teaching facilities. In addition to the criterion of staff to pupil ratios, he stressed the space per pupil in individual classrooms. He was of the opinion that few of the school's rooms could satisfactorily accommodate more than thirty pupils. In any case, it was his opinion that 'from the teaching point of view, a class should never exceed that number'. With an entry of 75 pupils, three forms had to be organised and, for a three stream Grammar School, he put the case for a staff of 24. The Inspector concerned recommended a compromise of 22.7. An assistant was also needed to service the increasing number of laboratories.

Side by side with the inspection a new *Instrument of Government* was being prepared for the management of the school. The governors now held office in accordance with *Instrument* No. 287 sealed September 28, 1953. It stipulated that the governing body was to consist of 'Four Foundation Governors (three co-opted and one appointed by the Hebdomadal Council of the University of Oxford) and eight representative governors of whom at least two shall be women, to be appointed by the Buckinghamshire County Council, of whom two shall be appointed on the nomination of the Divisional Executive'. Some new governors therefore appeared side by side with the new headmaster.

Continuous talk about lack of space turned eyes to the possible alternative uses of the garden of the headmaster's house, Miss Taffs' garden and the garden of Saxonia house in Turnfurlong (which was now Council property). The orchard was incorporated into the playing field – thereby eliminating the traditional practice of 'scrumping'. The inadequacy of the sports field was temporarily eased by the use of a field in Turnfurlong, but additional land in Wendover Way proved less acceptable. It lacked shelter and changing facilities of any kind and the erection of a prefabricated building led to immediate objection from the local residents. The situation was especially disappointing for soccer and rugby teams wishing to practise for Saturday matches. Not surprisingly, younger 'hopefuls' were often wooed away to play for the town teams.

There was a lack of accommodation at the school for the annual Speech Day. An experience with the Granada Cinema proved embarrassing. The governors, staff and other occupants of the stage had to choose between the blinding glare of the stage lights or lighting so subdued that they were only seen with difficulty from the auditorium. The Town Hall was the setting on November 26, 1953. At 10.30 p.m. on the same day a resident in Victoria Street saw smoke rising from the roof of the main school building. The fire appeared to spread by way of the wiring and, although it was only minutes later that the fire brigade arrived, the hall and physics laboratory were ablaze. Ironically all this happened on the same day that the Headmaster had been delivering a speech on the inadequacy of the very building. The school's difficulties were suddenly compounded. The event presaged a short-term disruption. But it was to have profound long-term advantages.

More than one pupil admits to having 'dissolved into tears' at the sight of the charred building, but it was not long before members of the sixth form were helping to salvage as much as possible from the debris.

The physics laboratory after the fire in 1953.

Letters of sympathy came to the Headmaster from all over the country. One was unusual. 'It is too much to hope', it began, 'that the promise made in 1904 that a second school for girls should ultimately be brought to fruition, but I suppose that it would seem a retrograde step today.' An inventory of equipment lost or damaged had to be prepared for the insurance claim (values change – the grand piano was listed at £36). Within five days classes which could be accommodated in unaffected buildings were back to normal. Temporary accommodation was provided in six classrooms at Queen's Park Secondary Modern School and in other rooms at the nearby Technical School. Walton Road traffic was held up by yet more unwelcome 'crocodiles'. The Local Education Authority lost no time in setting in motion the reinstatement of the building.

There was additional irony in the fact that in October 1953 the school's architect, Frederick Taylor, had handed over to the Education Committee his collection of plans and drawings covering much of the new school's history (he received a fee of 25 guineas). Within two months, an entire new series of plans had to be prepared at short notice for the reconstruction and conversion of the damaged buildings.

The reinstatement proceeded apace. The former hall was to be converted into a sixth form room and library, with simplified interior decoration and improved ventilation. The entire electrical installations of the school buildings and Headmaster's house were to be thoroughly inspected. Alternative heating was to be provided for the staff room following the closing of all chimneys. The contractors undertook to complete the restoration in twelve weeks. A bus load of well-disciplined workmen arrived daily from somewhere in outer London. The final forty-eight hours witnessed the arrival of a virtual army of painters and decorators so that the operation could be completed within the time schedule. There was a happy footnote to the disorganisation caused by the fire. It had no effect on the examination results.

A number of lesser decisions had to be taken about other damaged items. It was decided not to replace the old honours boards. Instead, the Chairman of Governors donated black leather-bound books in which names would be written and which were to be kept with the school trophies. A debt is owed to Dennis Lack for the exceptional calligraphy in which the record of honours was renewed. In due course, insurance was received for the war memorial, the honours boards, and the portraits of Sir Henry Lee and Henry Phillips. An artist was appointed to provide a copy of Sir Henry Lee's portrait in the National Portrait Gallery. No portrait of Henry Phillips was known to exist though money was set aside for a copy should one come to light. The Old Aylesburians provided a new sepia photograph of Thomas Osborne. Fortunately, Frederick Taylor's pleasing watercolour of the school entrance, which he had donated to the school, suffered no damage.

While the restoration of the old building brought much satisfaction, more excitement was engendered by the plans that were being drawn

Hurdling in 1952, the race between Messrs. Fitton and Wixon. David Wixon had a distinguished career in the Navy. He was in command of H.M.S. Drake at Devonport before his retirement.

The girls' tennis team c. 1955 (Angela Billingham seated left).

up for the construction of extensive new accommodation. By January 1954, permission had been given for the erection of a new hall with two 'green rooms', two biology laboratories and a physics laboratory. These were to be erected on the site of the tennis courts. A handsome memorial honouring Sir Henry Lee and Henry Phillips and listing the names of those who died during the two world wars was placed in the new hall. The buildings were opened formally on May 3, 1955 by the Chairman of Governors, Mrs. Paterson, with the Bishop of Oxford conducting a service of dedication. Trees were planted to commemorate the opening. They included the birch, the rowan and Mrs. Paterson's quince which

The start of the cross-country run c. 1958.

remain in the quadrangle. A curious error is to be found on the memorial. From whence derived the baronetcy ascribed to Sir Henry? Baronetcies were not introduced until 1611 – after his death. A cousin, Sir Henry Lee, was one of the first (DNB, 1892).

By 1954 the new Headmaster had sufficient time to look into other matters. He initiated a series of meetings with the parents of prospective pupils and during the first year visited Wendover, Aston Clinton, Waddesdon and Stoke Mandeville. A new set of rules was drawn up and circulated to staff, pupils and parents. A new school cap was provided for boys who had earned 'colours' on the sports field. Shortly afterwards, a paper on girls' uniforms was circulated. Twenty specific items of clothing were listed. It implied not inconsiderable expense for parents. The wearing of coloured hair ribbons, rings, bracelets and jewellery as well as expensive watches was proscribed. Further regulations had to be anticipated.

Such considerations were soon to be replaced by weightier matters. Not entirely without warning, it was reported at a meeting of the Foundation Governors (19/1/1956) that the County Council had reached a definite decision to create two single sex schools, the Foundation being attached to the boys' school. The decision was taken partly on the grounds of expediency and partly for economic reasons. It enabled the new school for girls to be 'got into the forward building list for 1957'. The full governors' meeting accepted the situation 'with reluctance', and it was no great comfort to be informed by the Local Education Authority that, if a third grammar school were needed in the future, it would be a mixed school. Most parents were unhappy with the decision. One made a vain attempt to encourage all parents to approach the Authority as a body. The debate even reached the House of Commons where the Minister for Education intimated that it was appropriate to have a school for girls. As C.G.S Furley wrote in an editorial for *The Aylesburian*, 'a town the name of which had only been synonymous with ducks ... suddenly hit the national press and radio.' A decision was reached by the spring that the new girls' school would be located on the old Grange site. Sketch plans of the new school and of associated extensions to the boys' school were reported (4/10/1957). Plans had to be made for the girls to move to the new premises in September 1959.

A new scheme for the Foundation had to be drafted as a result of the division of the school. The governors were unanimous that the Minister be asked 'to propound a new scheme with the Foundation Governors of the school as trustees and a separate clerk/treasurer'. The Foundation income was to be used for the benefit of the boys' school only. Scholarships and prizes were regarded as a suitable use for the income. In the event of any choice of beneficiary having to be made, preference should be given to boys from 'the ancient parishes of Aylesbury and Walton'. The relevant *Instrument of Government* No. 42845 was sealed March 24, 1960. It included a schedule of property. The new and smaller meeting of the trustees of the Aylesbury Grammar

School Foundation met for the first time on April 19, 1960.

The momentum of extra-curricular activity proceeded regardless of the prospective changes. *A Midsummer Night's Dream* received an award of merit from the Aylesbury Arts Festival. *Mary Rose* was the challenging choice of the Drama Society for the following year. The House Music Festival gained in stature with the expansion of the brass band from a quartet to 25 instrumentalists. Music camps at Shortenhills entered the programme. The Music Society had a memorable visit to Boosey and Hawkes, the publishers, and the Warwick Opera Group performed at the school.

School societies continued to extend the range of their visits. The biologists visited Flatford Mill: the scientists, the Royal Porcelain Works at Worcester. There were visits to Devon and Cornwall, Cheddar, Portsmouth, Hatfield House and the Tate Gallery.

Records continued to be broken at the annual Sports Day and a group of pupils went to the All England Sports at Plymouth. Boxing was revived with considerable success, with one competitor, David Oakley, narrowly losing in the All England and Welsh Finals at the Royal Albert Hall.

And, while the Headmaster pressed the need for new canteen facilities for pupils and staff, while school parties went off to Switzerland, Spain and Rome, and while the school's first television was loaned from Associated Rediffusion, a host of details had to be considered about the transitional arrangements. The transfer of staff and their special allowances had to be agreed. The salary scales of the 26 members of staff (nine of them women) had to be confirmed. For examination purposes alone, it was necessary to keep senior classes mixed in the short term. The future status of houses, societies and trophies had to be determined. Parents, too, had to be kept informed of the developments.

Ratepayers were reported by the local press as being disturbed by the costs involved. Even as the girders rose above the new girls' school there were lamentations over the division. For all concerned the final few months were charged with emotion. This was given expression at the memorable retirement party of the senior master Harry Deeming who, for many, was the embodiment of the school. The old was rung out and the new rung in at a gathering which brought together the governors and staffs of the two schools. For Aylesbury Grammar School, it was in a way a reversion to the situation as it was prior to 1907.

Material continues to flow in which might have been incorporated in the text had it arrived earlier. Some will find its way into the exhibition for the four hundredth anniversary of the school to be held at the County Museum in June and July of 1998.

This photograph of a school trip to Paris led by Maurice Severn in 1938 has been discovered by the publisher Peter Medcalf. He remembers that the excursion finished with a memorable (and very educational) visit to the Bal Tabarin nightclub in Montmartre.

Part 3

THE NEW SCHOOL

A NEW BEGINNING

It was not only the closure of a successful school which, although less than half a century old, had become a central feature in the life of the town. It was the fact that two new schools had to be created, neither of which was able to inherit the traditions of the old. In a way, it was easier for the High School for Girls. Under its first Headmistress Miss Joan Camp, at least it began life in new premises. For the Boys' Grammar School it was a matter of putting new wine into old bottles. If it had been realised how much construction work was to intrude upon the daily life of the school in the next few years, the prospect might have been viewed with considerable apprehension.

Adjustments were also called for in personal relationships. Staff who had worked together as a team, now found themselves divided between two institutions. All had to adjust to teaching in single sex schools. For some it was less agreeable than for others – some having deliberately chosen appointments in a co-educational establishment. A relatively large number of new colleagues had also to be absorbed in a short time into two institutions. Old allegiances, working partnerships and practices had to be replaced by new. The very sounds in the corridors were different. It was remarked that the departure of the girls was a 'high price to pay for silence'. 'The place has never seemed so quiet', lamented a pupil. 'The quality of the pranks certainly dminished', wrote Dennis Lack. 'The girls had supplied the imagination and left the boys to do the deeds.' No one was more important at this time than L.J. (as R. Lloyd-Jones came to be called). He swiftly adopted the mantle of Harry Deeming, carrying the values and ethos of the old school to the new.

It was not long before the Grammar School site was invaded by builders and demolition workers, drills and cement mixers as a pro-

The joint High School and Grammar School production of A Midsummer Night's Dream in 1960. David Briggs was largely responsible for the sets of this ambitious production.

gramme of 'major capital works' was set in motion. First came the Tower Block, the ground floor of which was ready for use in 1961. Five hundred boys were expected in the new school year. Not surprisingly, accommodation was not ready, so once again it was a matter of using the dreaded temporary facilities of the vacated Technical School. 'Deep seated irritation' was probably an understatement of the reaction. The woodwork and metalwork rooms might be completed in 1962, but it was another year before the gymnasium was roofed in its final form (the water tanks in it burst during the Arctic winter a year later). The canteen at the eastern end of the gymnasium was soon ready for use and the car park in front of the school was opened. With the four-storied Tower Block completed in 1963 it seemed that things were on the move.

Meanwhile, the so-called 'phasing plan' for the completion of the promised buildings experienced its third revision. By 1964, six laboratories were at last available and the completion of extensions to the hall in 1965 enabled the Headmaster to report 'a great boost to morale' as a milestone in building was reached. Even a caretaker's house was acquired in Walton Road.

But, at least, thanks to Henry Phillips' gift, the boys Grammar School was able to acquire a feature that was the envy of every other educational establishment in town. The sale of two of the Foundation's fields in Stocklake, which had been bought in 1715, yielded the (then) princely sum of £26,625. The trustees were unanimous that it should be used for the provision of a covered swimming pool. J.H. Cox, of Architects Partnership, was asked to provide a design scheme with estimated costs. Metrication having arrived, the 25m pool, with heating, chlorination and filtration systems, changing rooms and toilets, was put at £28,000. The possibility of an arrangement with the High School was discussed and it was hoped that the County Council might agree to maintenance costs. Discussions about the estimates continued for the better part of a year before a contract to go ahead was agreed at the price of £30,000 (11/6/1965). The deficit was not easily found. The County Council and Harding's Charity together provided £2,000. A possible loan from Lloyds Bank, using Manor Farm as security, was turned down. In order to raise the necessary funds, the possibility of selling the headmaster's house to the County Council was proposed. Alternatively, the Council might be asked to take the house in lieu of accepting responsibility for the remainder of the costs.

Negotiations were now entered into with the High School. Its governors were approached (1/5/1965) to see 'if they could give an undertaking that they would not make an application for a grant towards a separate pool if a large grant was made towards the Grammar School pool on the grounds that it would also be used by girls from the High School.'

As a result, the County Council finally agreed to accept the running costs and care of the pool on completion of its construction in November 1967. The construction company agreed to treat the deficit as a loan (against the security of Manor Farm) with interest at eight per cent until such time as capital was forthcoming. So, protective netting having been placed over the windows against stray cricket balls – and, later, golf balls, – what might have been appropriately called the Henry Phillips Pool (but wasn't) became a distinguishing feature of the school. Mrs. Paterson gave three silver cups to be used as swimming trophies.

Side by side with all these activities, the teaching programme expanded as new facilities came into use. Trainee teachers from the Department of Education at Oxford had been a regular feature of the school since the First World War. In the middle 1950s there were as many as eight at the same time. They began to disappear a decade later. Part-time teachers seemed to be difficult to find: so, too, cleaners (it was a time of full employment). UCCA came into being in 1962 to simplify the system of university applications. A sixth form council was established the following year and provided a useful forum in which sensitive issues could be smoothed out. In the early 1960s three new staff members were appointed – Ian Roe, Brian Roberts and Robin Pike who were eventually to 'clock up' more than a century of service between them. Provision had to be made for a new trend in the sixth form, where the social sciences claimed increasing interest. Foreign field trips multiplied – Cannes, Montreux, Perpignan, St. Malo, Annecy, Lugano. There were also exchange visits through the Anglo-Austrian Society and with a school in Douai. Winter sports holidays began in 1966.

By 1966, it had become increasingly necessary to find a solution to the problem of transport for schools established on the Walton Road site.

The shape of things to come - the beginning of work on the tower block and the sixth form block. When the last of the First World War army huts was removed to make way for the tower, a box of old books was found. They were said to have included Latin and Greek texts, some of seventeenth century origin. There is no record as to what happened to them. (Is it possible that they were the residue of the Reverend Ralph Gladman's gift as noted on page 15?).

The County Authority took the matter in hand and the first lay-by for buses was established in Turnfurlong. In 1966, the school also qualified for the appointment of a matron.

Perhaps the prolonged appearance of large areas of the school as a building site discouraged the concern of many of the boys about their own appearances. At any rate a new initiative on school uniform sought the support of parents from 1961 onwards (the parents were described as 'willing, but weak allies'). School caps, for a while veritable symbols of athleticism, were being slowly demoted. First, they were made optional for the sixth form. Then, because fifth form boys seemed to gain in height and maturity before entering the sixth form, the option was extended to them. In 1964, the wearing of duffle coats (except dark blue) was proscribed as were coats of plastic and leather. Attention was first directed to hair styles in 1962 and two years later long hair was being dealt with 'discreetly'. Regulation plain grey trousers were not allowed to be 'drainpiped'. Plain grey V-necked pullovers were permitted beneath the black blazers. Leather shoes were expected to be 'polished'. Rings were not to be worn. Fountain pens had been around for a long time, but ink was still needed. Ball type pens (which were unreliable and had a disastrous capacity for leaking) were not permitted until 1965.

So, appropriately dressed, members of the school travelled as far afield as Berlin, Italy and Austria. Individual forms had excursions to Edinburgh, Peterborough, Ely, Guildford and Bristol. The geographers had field trips to North Wales and Derbyshire, while the Scientific Society took in Baddesley Colliery and the Harwell Atomic Research Establishment.

Sixth Form Volunteer Service groups continued their work at Stoke Mandeville Hospital, The Chestnuts Old People's Home and St. John's Hospital at Stone.

For those who looked back to the 'sixties', they were a 'golden age' for the Dramatic Society. New halls were available for ambitious joint productions of Anouilh's *The Lark*, Tchekhov's *Three Sisters* and T.S. Eliot's *Murder in the Cathedral*. There were many rewarding performances. Caesar and Cleopatra, Ophelia and Beatrice, Becket and Benedict – and Juliet's nurse are all still very much alive in the memory of George Butcher, English master at the time.

There were fears that the remarkable musical standards achieved in the life of the school would be difficult to maintain following the retirement of C.A.G. Pope. But highly talented music teachers were found and the tradition of performing substantial works continued. Among them were Coleridge Taylor's *Hiawatha*, Benjamin Britten's *St. Nicholas*, Vivaldi's *Gloria* and Parry's *Blest Pair of Sirens*.

On the academic front, thanks to the initiative of Arthur Taylor, the Lipscomb Society was born. It proved immensely stimulating, and influenced a generation of young historians some of whom have risen to prominence in local history circles. Nor did its members fail to seize the opportunity of linking up with the Buckinghamshire Archaeological Society, whose sponsored digs they visited on Ivinghoe Beacon and Bedgrove Farm. The Lipscomb Society was succeeded by the Verney

Aylesbury Grammar School Squash Team, 1976.

Society which was formed when War Games became fashionable. Encounters between Cavalier and Roundhead were fought out on table top in the library, and sites from battlefields during the Civil War were visited.

A contrasting sign of the times were the burglaries reported in 1961, 1962 and 1963. Schoolboy vandals entered and damaged the school premises on several occasions until volunteer members of staff undertook a spell of night duty and successfully handed over a number of culprits to the police. All this paled into insignificance for one pupil whose father stumbled on the hide-out of the Great Train Robbers at Leatherslade Farm. Ian Beckett recalls the excitement in a class held in a Walton Road annexe when a 'Black Maria' drove by daily carrying the robbers themselves to court.

A TIME OF FULFILMENT

Keith Smith took over from Lionel Tidmarsh at a strategic time in the spring term in 1967. He came from a deputy headship at Theale Grammar School in Berkshire. He was the first head not to occupy the headmaster's house. The Foundation Governors were of the opinion that it was not a suitable residence but, that with limited alterations, it could provide satisfactory accommodation for sixth form teaching. In fact, the new Headmaster entered the school at what was relatively speaking not an inauspicious time financially for the school Foundation. Cash funds had been accumulating and the Chairman of Governors (27/11/1967) proposed that a number of worthwhile projects might be supported. It did not take K.D. Smith long to produce a list, together with estimated costs.

Principal among the items were squash courts (four were completed in 1968 with a common spectators' gallery), a standard indoor rifle range (completed in 1969), funds for the school library, a minibus and a grant for the sixth form house. The County Council agreed to cover the costs of maintaining and running the minibus, plus licensing and insurance costs. Inevitably, the capital outlay exceeded the estimates; but, nothing daunted, the list was soon extended in order to double the provisions in the audio-active room and – unsuccessfully – to equip a room for pottery

Aylesbury Grammar School Rugby Seven, 1977.

and sculpture. 'All weather pitches' were suggested, but they too were passed over until more favourable times. It was necessary to seek approval from the Charity Commissioners for all expenditure by the Foundation. Their agreement stipulated that capital expenditure could be recouped over a thirty or sixty year period, subject to the deduction of one fifteenth of the amount spent. Among other items acquired was a telescope from an amateur astronomer in Aylesbury, though a dome on a base had to be provided out of school funds. Two boys immediately set about making a video of the moon's surface.

Although K.D. Smith found a relatively strong Foundation, the finances available from the County Council were seriously inadequate. His first task was to persuade the Education Officers that extra money should be made available for equipment and books for the new Nuffield Science courses in physics, chemistry and biology that had been introduced throughout the school. Within a week of appointment, he also persuaded the Chief Education Officer, Roy Harding, to provide a minor works project to create four housemaster rooms. This was the first necessary step in changing the bias of pastoral care in the school from a form master system to one based on the house organisation.

While, for the time being, the school might have overcome most of its problems of space, there were never enough resources to meet the demands for equipment. Expectations had been building up during the 1960s and it was not long before every meeting of the Foundation Governors saw on the agenda items amounting to thousands of pounds. This was a reflection of the fact that schools were entering a new age with rapidly changing knowledge and textbooks, with new subjects and the corresponding need for new facilities. The 1970s brought with them a different problem in the shape of inflation which increased difficulties in forecasting costs.

Having overcome the demise of the mixed school in the 1950s and the establishment of a new school – physically and pedagogically – in the 1960s, a new challenge became manifest in the 1970s. As early as May, 1965, 'the potential of unpalatable decisions' for the school was hinted at in a governors' meeting. The following year, plans for the possible 'comprehensivisation' of the County were placed on the agenda for the first time. In 1973, K.D. Smith invited Grammar School headteachers from throughout the county to sign a letter to all county councillors giving the reasons they should consider before abandoning a successful system in favour of a politically imposed change with no additional resources provided. Although all Divisional Executives had reluctantly accepted this change, the County Council reversed this decision and decided to keep the status quo. Parent governors especially Jean Belger and John Alder were especially active in leading the eventual fight to retain the selective system in Buckinghamshire. The situation came to a head in September 1978 when a special meeting of the Foundation Governors was called in

K.D. Smith, O.B.E., M.A. Cantab., Headmaster 1967-1992, receiving Sir Peter Gadsden, Lord Mayor of London, on the occasion of his visit to the school in 1979.

the light of a 'government directive that all schools had to become comprehensive.' The alternatives for the school to the 12-18 comprehensive model were the conversion of the school into a mixed sixth form college of more than a thousand pupils or into an independent fee-paying institution. The Headmaster favoured the solution of a sixth form college with two colleges fed from 12-16 comprehensive schools. The second sixth form college would be based on the Aylesbury College and Sir Henry Floyd site and provide a wide range of mainly vocational courses.

It was clear that the Foundation had insufficient funds to contemplate becoming an independent school. The Foundation Governors resolved that the school did not wish to become independent and the staff were advised accordingly. The possibility of the school becoming a sixth form college caused considerable anxiety at other schools in the town, especially at Aylesbury High School. There were sighs of relief when, a year later, the County Education Authority (which in any case had been reluctant to force the issue) reported that following the General Election any proposals to make the school comprehensive 'appeared to have been lain on one side.' The Headmaster could scarcely believe it. In his Speech Day address he called 1979 'the year of the temporary reprieve'.

While the debate on comprehensivisation was proceeding, other important developments were taking place across the entire school spectrum. First, there were pastoral issues. A new tutorial system was introduced in September 1967, with a house tutor staying with his tutees as they progressed up the school. Junior, Middle and Sixth Form 'Councils' were elected which met with the Headmaster to discuss ideas about life in school and extra-curricular activities. Following a request from pupils, joint school dances with the High School were started at sixth and fifth form levels and, with the help of volunteer staff and senior pupils, continued to flourish. Following lively debate with the staff, a decision was reached to call boys by their Christian names instead of their surnames (in the 'old days' staff had sometimes even called them by their nicknames). The increasingly contentious cap began to disappear at the same time.

Beyond the school, K.D. Smith was responsible for the establishment of Aylesbury Youth Action, of which he was to remain Chairman into his retirement. The purpose of Youth Action was to provide opportunities in training young people to understand and help those in need as well as to bring together some 500 boys and girls from the secondary schools of Aylesbury to work together on various projects. It was a pastoral activity at another level which tied in with a number of the school's extra-curricular activities.

Secondly, the curriculum was expanded. Provision was made on the science side for all boys to carry out a science craft project, and the Craft Department became an Applied Science and Technology Department. The development greatly impressed Sir James Hamilton of the Department of Education and Science when he visited the school. In the teaching of physics, chemistry and biology, Nuffield methods were adopted. The 32-seater Cybervox language laboratory was working at full pressure. The increasing use of audio-visual teaching must have played a part in an inspector's report in 1974 which stated that the standard of French teaching by Ian Roe was the highest he had experienced in his inspections throughout the country. Spanish was introduced as an additional foreign language. A new interest in Latin emerged after a change to a more modern approach. Greek was made available as an option at both 'O' and 'A' level and a classical civilisation course was provided for all pupils in their first year at the school.

In 1969, the school began experimenting with computers. It was one of the first fifty schools in the country selected to try out a specially devised computer programme for school timetables. However, Peter Cass the school timetabler soon realised that it was not sufficiently sophisticated to cope with an increasingly complicated timetable. It was, however, useful as a checking device to eliminate mistakes.

A room equipped with programmed learning machines was used in teaching mathematics and, although this proved useful especially in remedial teaching, the lack of new programmes and replacement machines led to its gradual disuse.

Thirdly, an important policy decision was taken not to have a minimum standard of entry to the sixth form, but to admit according to the likely benefit that a boy would derive from the experience. As a result a much higher number of pupils from secondary modern schools were admitted than in any other local school – a procedure strongly supporting the county selective system.

Fourthly, a number of steps were taken to raise individual standards. A system of 'merit marks' was introduced to junior forms, where progress prizes were substituted for 'second' prizes. Merit holidays were established, while those whose work effort or conduct did not merit a holiday were supervised at school by the Headmaster with the help of senior staff. A strong third year sixth form was created to allow for Oxford and Cambridge entry as well as the retake of 'A' levels.

The increase in school numbers also affected the old-established school house system. In 1975, Lee was added to the existing four. When asked about its origin, one of the first members of the house was overheard to remark in the school playground, 'We only happened this year.' The sixth house – Paterson – 'happened' in the 1980s.

In 1974 the age of admission was lifted from eleven to twelve and the two following intakes of boys witnessed yet again the intrusive builders. They had completed major additions to the school by 1977 – a lecture theatre to seat 400 pupils built with help from the Harding trustees, nine science laboratories, an applied science workshop area, a new library and library office, a sixth form common room, an audio-visual resources room, a number of much appreciated head of department rooms and sixth form classrooms.

By 1982, it could be claimed that all boys in the first two years of the school had been introduced to computer studies. Shortly afterwards, a further building programme together with a generous grant for computers from the trustees of the William Harding Charity brought the realisation of a computer centre nearer. It was opened by Sir Timothy Raison in 1983 and described by *The Times* as providing 'the best computer facilities of any school in the United Kingdom'. Boys who had set up the satellite tracking station with its 'Short Wave Club' were particularly appreciative. Others won competitions as a result – Pat Tylor for his program to produce a musical score for the partially sighted: Simon Jones, for his program on geographical contours.

A further building programme enabled a specialist geography and geology block to be provided on the edge of the school field and parallel to the swimming pool. Geography had always been a popular subject at the school and by now geology was proving to be almost as attractive as a sixth form option. A government inspection of the subject brought

120

The Public Speaking and Debating Team that won The Observer Mace in 1992.

high commendation of the provision which was still unusual in secondary education.

At the time of his retirement, when he was succeeded as first deputy head by Harry Helliwell, R. Lloyd-Jones wrote a contribution for *The Aylesburian* in which he contrasted the unbelievably lean (and hungry) situation in the school when he was appointed in 1946 with its expansive and resilient mood three decades later. With the ghost of comprehensivisation laid, the school faced with confidence the educational reforms that were to come thick and fast in the 1980s.

Ian Roe was appointed second deputy head and later Chris Williams and David Bassett became deputies, enabling each deputy to have one section of the school. Separate assemblies were introduced for the Junior, Middle and Upper School three days a week with house assemblies on Tuesdays and Thursdays.

The cricket team that toured Trinidad and Tobago in 1995, organised by Simon Winman and David Gajadharsingh.

The first administrative change to affect the school was the reorganisation of the governing body. Following a year of consultations with the governors, a new instrument for the government of voluntary controlled schools in Buckinghamshire came into effect in September 1985. Its principal recommendations referred to the constitution of the governing body, disqualifications for membership, the quorum and arrangements for the transitional period from the old to the new system. Henceforth, the governing body was to consist of five foundation governors, five representative governors from the County Council, two elected parent governors, two teacher governors and three co-opted governors (including one from the District Council), together with the headmaster. There was general satisfaction with the arrangement. The election of parent governors generated considerable interest when hustings took place in the main lecture theatre. Canon Adeane Byndard, whose many years of devoted service to the town and the school made him a popular figure, presided as chairman over the new body.

The next reform impinged more fundamentally on the school – legislation which introduced Grant Maintained Status as an alternative to Local Management. The governors and parents had the option of retaining their association with the local authority or opting out and becoming accountable to the Department of Education through its Funding Agency for Schools. The initial decision to maintain the status quo was not difficult to reach, but henceforth governors were required annually to decide whether or not to ballot parents on the value and viability of turning to Grant Maintained Status.

Local Management undoubtedly gave a new flexibility to the operation of a school, but it was accompanied by new responsibilities. Principal among these was the management of finances. It need hardly be said that Aylesbury Grammar School had no difficulty in this area, but it was confronted with one consequence of past good housekeeping. The wise accumulation of reserves for a 'rainy day' or an important future project was a practice which did not chime with the annual budgeting of national and local authorities, and it was necessary to deal with this issue prudently. The principal task of the Personnel and Finance Committee was henceforth to be the maintenance of staff in the face of all too regular cost-cutting. The maintenance of buildings of diverse age and character, especially those constructed during leaner years, was a continuing problem. Heating and lighting in particular called for urgent rationalisation. An energy consultant, who must have cast a despairing eye over the scattered buildings and their antiquated fittings, nevertheless provided an impressive solution. Increasingly stringent health and safety regulations called for insurance which, happily, could be 'bought in' from the local authority. It was also one of the requirements of the new system of management that an annual report should be submitted to parents and dealt with at a special meeting.

The third reform struck at the core of the teaching programme – the introduction of a National Curriculum. It called for major modifications of the syllabus – and consequently the timetable – throughout the school. For a while the old curriculum and the new had to be run in tandem. Adjustments were more difficult because of the diversity of subjects cultivated in the school. Patience and tolerance were stretched. Fortunately, they were less disturbed by another sensitive requirement – the introduction of the teacher appraisal scheme.

It was ironical that, as the ghost of comprehensivisation was laid to rest, outstanding examination results were being achieved. In the early 1980s, the number of places and the number of scholarships and exhibitions awarded by Oxford and Cambridge proved to be one of the highest for any state school in the country and even better than those achieved by many of the leading schools in the independent sector.

There were similar achievements in the sporting field. The school rugby team was one of the strongest in the country and competed in most of the inter-school national seven-a-side tournaments. For many years they more than held their own against the arch-rival the Royal Grammar School, High Wycombe. The school cricket team was unbeaten for a number of years and, in both cricket and rugby, the school provided more members of the County junior side than any other school. For two years in succession there were wins in the County Open Hockey Tournament. The school badminton team had entered the National Schools Tournament, and in 1990 the under 15 tennis team won the South of England Championship. There were successes in the National Schools Sailing Association's Championship and the British Schools Rifle Shooting League (which was coached by Stewart Armour, a former holder of the Grand Challenge Trophy at Bisley and a coach of the England shooting team). But it was the squash teams that provided the climax. By the mid-eighties they had been national champions six times in nine years. Meanwhile, thanks to the Local Education Authority, the school acquired the sports ground of Hazell, Watson and Viney. It might be ten minutes walk away, subject to intrusive local residents and difficult to maintain, but at least it doubled the school's grass area. However, even before the improvement that it brought, the school had established a reputation as one of the best in the country for its games standard – thanks to the devotion of Brian Roberts and many members of staff.

Joint dramatic and musical performances with the High School continued to flourish – Lehar as well as Gilbert and Sullivan being presented for the first time. A production of *Dr. Faustus* provided a high point, with nearly a hundred participants and with an excess of dry ice to add to the excitement. Not entirely unnoticed, Kenneth Williams, Patrick Moore and Roald Dahl slipped in to entertain favoured groups. A new experience was provided by the Thames sailing barge *Thalatta*, with the traditional concluding mud baths. A winter exchange visit with a school in Quebec City was another novelty and for several years the school sent a party on the County organised Mediterranean cruise, visiting Greece, Egypt, Turkey and Israel.

The school did not neglect the needs of others. The school council representatives decided to give regular support to two fund-raising projects. The first was to provide funds for St. John's Hospital at Stone after the boys had seen a report showing that this was the least supported of the hospitals in the Aylesbury Vale. The second was to provide machines for St. Luke's Hospital at Kasupe in Malawi. A former head boy used his GAP year to help in the hospital and thus encouraged further support by his first-hand accounts of the needs of the patients. The profits of a variety of ambitious musical activities under the baton of John Brown helped a number of local causes. The barbershop group – later to become *Doctor's Orders* – made its first appearance in straw boaters and

Doctor's Orders, the school barbershop group.

striped waistcoats. Nor did the silver jubilee of the New School pass without celebrations. A weekend of activities was shared with the High School. Members of the school regularly took part in a variety of sponsored events to raise money for both the school and various charities. For four years running, the school swimming pool was made available for Aylesbury pupils to take part in a sponsored swim to raise money for the Aylesbury Rotary Club's campaign to help Rotary International to provide vaccines to eradicate polio and other major world diseases.

Enthusiasm is infectious. It was readily communicated to the Parent Teacher Association which had been formed in 1968 and which organised an annually increasing number of the fund raising activities. The PTA Committee also met regularly with the Headmaster to plan a programme of parents' evenings when the school could explain to parents the teaching methods, opportunities and organisation and also invite speakers from universities and other bodies.

In 1992, Keith Smith retired, leaving the school at the height of its achievements. His talents and energy were immediately sought by a number of national institutions. For his contributions to the school, the town, the county and indeed the nation at large, he was awarded the OBE in 1993.

It did not seem that it would be easy to find a successor but, from among the large number of applicants, one rapidly emerged in the senior master, Ian Roe. It was an appointment favoured by staff and governors alike, but unusual in that it was internal and that the new headmaster was a graduate of one of the newer universities. It was his good fortune to be able to continue a tradition which in his previous position he had helped to create. Stability and continuity were important when so many changes were being forced upon the school from without. The almost immediate appointment of Christopher Tarrant to the headship of Wilson's Grammar School in Surrey provided the opportunity to appoint a deputy head – Richard Kemp, from his post as Senior Adviser in the County.

Nor was it long before the school was challenged by the looming shadow of an inspection. A new acronym, OFSTED, entered the educational vocabulary. The Local Education Authority might issue comforting circulars declaring that there was no cause for alarm, but the arrival

Ian Roe, BA, appointed Headmaster in 1992.

of a team of fifteen inspectors who were to be around the school for a week or more could hardly fail to generate a measure of stress. They took over the Board Room complete with a barrowload of school policy documents, their own computer and kettle, and could be seen in school from 7 a.m. to 8 p.m. making their judgements. Parents were called to an open meeting to give their views on the school and questionnaires were issued to everyone. Paradoxically, the high rating that the school had received in national press surveys was inclined to increase rather than reduce apprehension. One member of the languages staff confessed to feeling 'washed out' at the end of the first day of inspection – not because he had been visited but because he had spent the day waiting for the door handle on the classroom to turn. In the event, within its highly stylised format, the report congratulated the school as being one of the best inspected during the year. At a later ceremony the Chairman of Governors, John Paterson, the Headmaster, staff, head boy and deputy head boy received a plaque from the Minister for Education commemorating the school's nomination by Her Majesty's Chief Inspector as being 'outstandingly successful.'

The curriculum continued to develop and the school was in the fore-front of those adopting the new modular 'A' level courses – and with great success. The choice of subjects continued to meet the demand of modern youth with computer science, business studies and communication studies all attracting enthusiasts. Results continued to climb to record percentages with over 96% pass rates at GCSE and 'A' level. In computer science in 1996 the school obtained four out of the top five results from over 4,000 students. Ben John obtained the highest marks of all candidates in both his physics and chemistry 'A' level papers and two students reached the national press with six 'A' grades at 'A' level each. By now the school was appearing on the front page of *The Times* in national league tables, coming twenty-fifth out of all schools for its 'A' level results.

It is a tribute to the teaching staff that, with the additional requirements crowding into the syllabus (not least education concerning sex and drugs) and, with the increasing load of paper work, there was no slackening in the area of extra-curricular activity. When the first *Directory of Societies, Clubs and Extra-Curricular Activity* was printed in 1993, it identified 33 in the Junior School, 33 in the Middle School and 28

The Jazz Band consists of some fifty instrumentalists. Under the direction of Nicholas Care, it came second in the 1995 Daily Telegraph Central Television Jazz Band of the Year Competition.

in the Sixth Form. The well-established Duke of Edinburgh's Award Scheme and Youth Action were to retain their appeal. A jazz band now complemented the school orchestra. The War Games Society continued to attract recruits. A sixth form Young Enterprise group established its own company in association with managers from the Equitable Life Assurance Society and other local companies – both a consequence of, and a stimulus to, the highly popular business studies course in the curriculum.

Schemes of work shadowing and community service were introduced for sixth form pupils. Two-day visits to local institutions helped to meet the professional curiosity of potential medics, lawyers, engineers and others. Pupils also began to undertake regular visits to local primary schools to help impart the skills of information technology, sport, music and drama to junior pupils.

The yearly round of house competitions was enhanced by a House Art Festival. Three hundred entries could be expected from all year groups to cover the display boards and tables which filled the hall. The House Music Festival, organised entirely by senior pupils, adapted to modern musical styles and tastes with the jazz band and barbershop influence being strongly felt.

At the same time, eyes were being turned to the wider world. It was exciting for boys to join with the British Schools Exploring Society's expeditions to Iceland, North Norway and North Sweden, but it was more rewarding to run an independent expedition to Costa Rica. And it was a long haul from Tom Bourdillon's talk on the ascent of Everest in 1953 to the school's own Karakorum Expedition of 1997. For a cricket team to go to Trinidad and Tobago in 1995 or a rugby team to South Africa in 1998 would have been beyond the imaginings of boys a generation previously. This did not mean that local visits were neglected. Martin Middleton initiated a residential visit for all year-eight pupils at Irthlingborough in Northamptonshire. Here, they were involved in night walks, abseiling from a tower and raft building for a lakeside challenge. All proved hugely popular.

Joint activities with the High School started to blossom with activity days for junior year groups. The most notable took place in 1996 with 360 year-nine boys and girls visiting the Royal Engineers near Sandhurst to carry out a day's problem solving activities. The lower sixth forms of the two schools began to meet annually for a two-day industrial conference which was always well supported by managers from local companies. Joint dances, operas, plays, debates and some general studies classes were all initiated by a liaison committee from the two schools. Another innovation was the local newsletter produced by members of the school, the High School and the Grange School for local residents and neighbours.

The level of participation in sporting activities continued to develop with the advent of Paul Dean as Head of Physical Education. The school added football to its range of sports and soon the under sixteen team reached the semi-final of the county football cup, while under the guidance of Ashley Robson the first eleven became County Champions. The school was declared a centre of excellence in tennis by the LTA follow-

The computer room in action.

ing its remarkable run of victories at the regional level of both the under-thirteen and under-fifteen age groups. The school strengthened its systems of recognition for sport and the arts by awarding Junior and Middle Colours and Senior Half Colours for sport, and Junior and Senior Honours badges for the Arts. Meanwhile county badges for sporting excellence were introduced by the County Council and in the year 1995 the school was awarded thirteen badges. The County Council also inaugurated an award to teachers for services to sport. The first award was made to Brian Roberts who for 32 years had done so much to raise standards in the school.

As its four hundredth anniversary approached, Aylesbury Grammar School had become a community of rather more than 1,100 members – ten times the number of Henry Phillips' foundation. A budget of some

£2½ million a year was being received by way of the Local Education Authority, with intermittent capital grants for particular purposes. As with all educational institutions in Aylesbury, substantial capital grants have also been received from the William Harding Charitable Trust. Indeed, the trustees have played the role of a latter day Henry Phillips and it is a pity that there is no portrait of Harding that could look out from these pages. Modest returns are still derived from the investments and rents of Phillips' foundation, while income from the John Mason Raven fund – an endownment established in memory of a former foundation governor – is earmarked for special equipment needs.

Substantial annual contributions have also been raised by the hardworking and loyal Parent Teacher Association. As the Association approached its thirtieth anniversary its spirit of enterprise seemed more lively than ever. The voluntarily run school uniform shop flourished under the commercial expertise of its founder Jo Dennis, a former chairman of the PTA. An annual art exhibition and sale, inaugurated by the parents and supported by the cheerful organisation of Deputy Head Chris Williams, was to become one of the most notable in the area. The school fête, the craft fair and supper quizzes were to prove as profitable as they were popular.

As with all educational institutions in the 1990s, it became increasingly common to look for support from local industry. An example of the response was provided by the Charitable Fund of Equitable Life which paid for the refurbishment of the school library.

In late 1996, the school launched its Four Hundredth Anniversary Appeal with three special evenings for parents and a handsome brochure, sponsored by the National Westminster Bank, was widely circulated. The principal purpose of the appeal was to equip and furnish the newly acquired Wynne Jones units – the only buildings on land contiguous with the school that would allow expansion. They were accessible from the school playground and were planned to house a technology suite and a new Art and Ceramics Department. Such facilities were to become more critical with the advent of an 11+ examination in 1999 and the consequential increase in pupil numbers.

Fortunately there had been no neglect of the school environment in the face of the pressure to make more intensive use of the site and to

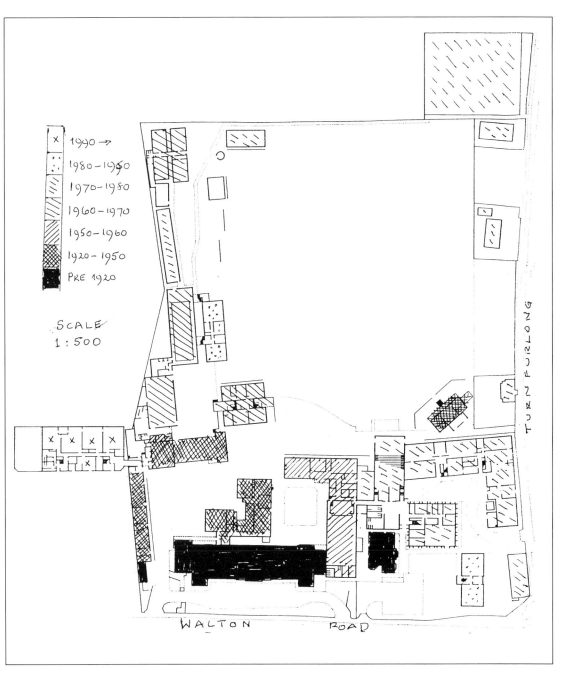

The expansion of the school premises (base plan by Director of Architecture and Property Services).

increase buildings on it. A special committee under the chairmanship of Jackie Brooker was established in 1992 to brighten the school's environment with plants, pictures, co-ordinated colour schemes and new areas of seating. The school also set up its own cleaning company, successfully bidding for the contract in the open market – and helping the school's budget in the process.

At the beginning of 1997, the Department of Education announced that Aylesbury Grammar School had been granted Technology College status. This was a considerable feather in the school's cap, only 150 schools nationally having been granted this special status. Links had already been established with a number of sponsoring companies, both local and national. With matched funding from the Department for Education and Employment, it was now possible to considerably enhance the facilities in technology, science and information technology. In addition to providing pupils with modern equipment, the establishment of special relationships with commercial companies enabled school work to be more closely involved with problems encountered in the world of employment. This pioneering venture was to prove especially stimulating to pupils.

The Old School, the Mixed School and the New School have been essentially different concepts. Each has served the town and the Vale in its distinctive way during the last century. At the same time, from being the only secondary school in the town, Aylesbury Grammar School has become one among a number. Though there may be an element of truth in it, *Primus inte pares* in this educational fellowship may sound somewhat pretentious. With four hundred years behind it, better perhaps to write *Veterrimus inte pares* – oldest among equals.

FLOREAT AYLESBURIA

As a charitable foundation the 'Free and Endowed' Aylesbury Grammar School is unique among schools in the town. It has a distinct legal status. In 1715, the 'inheritance' of landed property was invested in the hands of the trustees for 'a term of five hundred years.' The Aylesbury Grammar School Foundation, a registered charity number 310626, is governed by a scheme dated 24 March 1960, No 24845. In fact, the historic status of the school is of little consequence in the day-to-day running of its affairs. Nor, in reality, does it affect the relationships between the school and the Local Educational Authority, with which the governors – foundation, parent and nominated – have maintained cordial relations.

Longer-term planning has not been a strategy in which either the local authority or the governing body has engaged or has been able to engage until more recent years. The irony is that, as fast as planning strategies have been conceived, they have been made obsolete by the rapid changes in the educational structure that has been imposed at national level. Reforms have tended increasingly to become punctuation marks rather than milestones in the life of the school. Since the mixed school was opened, the steadily increasing demand for places has resulted in the piecemeal development of the school premises. The consequent accumulation of buildings of disparate age, character and quality is to a large extent the product of short-term extemporisation. As a result, the buildings fail to make the best of the restricted site, are unavoidably inefficient in their demands upon time and energy, and lack flexibility for use. And, overarching the entire situation, is the fact that the total space of the Walton Street site is inadequate for a school of so many pupils. Ironically, there is one inadequacy which repeats the situation in the old school of a century ago – the lack of a suitable sports field and the need to use inconvenient off-site facilities.

Sport used to be a means of binding together the successive generations which passed through the school. After the establishment of the mixed school there were keenly contested annual matches between teams of old boys – later also old girls – and resident pupils. An Old Aylesburian Association was established by the Headmaster at the outset. It mustered a fair number of recruits annually. Football and hockey matches in winter, cricket matches and tennis tournaments in summer between past and present Aylesburians encouraged rapport between the generations. The majority of school leavers found employment in the town and its surrounding area, while the small number who went on to institutions of higher education returned regularly to parents and relations. The experiences of the Second World War tended to reduce the continuity of the links, while the post-war increase in the size of the school resulted in a less closely-knit community. The division of the school caused a break between those who had belonged to the old Mixed School and the boys who entered what was to all intents and purposes a new institution. Pupils leaving the new school did not fit into the Old Aylesburian Association and an attempt to create a new organisation for them started with a promising supper party of 85, but thereafter declined. Perhaps the spirit of the time and the new social conditions that were coming about also hampered the maintenance of an alumnus organisation. From universities and other institutions former pupils began to migrate nation-wide and world-wide. Family mobility also increased. The atmosphere generated by historic premises, old-established traditions or customs – even minor icons such as badges and school colours – appears to play a part in creating a continuing sense of belonging. All this results in the fact that there are plenty of schools of lesser distinction where alumnus associations continue to flourish. Ultimately, perhaps, it is the dedication of honorary officers such as Joy Waters over a long period of time that matters most of all. And such people are born, not made.

Had there been an alumnus organisation it might have been easier to compile a fuller account of former members of the school who have contributed to its national standing. Two Old Aylesburians have been elected to the House of Commons. (Lewis) John Edwards was the first to hold office at the national level in a trade union, to enter parliament (as Labour member for Brighouse and Spenborough) and to become a Privy Councillor. He also served as President of the Consultative Assembly of the Council of Europe. Peter Rost was the second to enter parliament (as Conservative member for South-East Derbyshire), and probably the first of a number of Old Aylesburians to become a Freeman of the City of London. Angela Billingham (née Case) was the first to be elected to the European Parliament at Strasbourg, as Labour member for Northampton. A number of university chairs have been filled by former pupils, the first in 1963. At least three 'old boys' have been invited to provide entries for *Who's Who* and at least one 'old girl' has an entry in *Who's Who World of Women*. A president of the Cambridge Union is recorded and Crockfords has a sprinkling of entries. A number of foreign doctorates have been awarded as well as membership of foreign academies, including the European Academy. Fellowship of the British Academy has been achieved twice, but not of the Royal Society. The Colonial Service has recruited from the school in the past. Medicine has always attracted a number of former pupils, but only more recently have any been called to the Bar. Headmasters and headmistresses keep the educational flag flying. Roy Farran must claim the most distinguished war record with DSO, MC and Croix de Guerre. His book *Winged Dagger* must be the most exciting publication by an Old Aylesburian. The Cranwell Sword of Honour was achieved by a former pupil while the ranks of the Royal Air Force's *Red Arrows* were entered by Robert Last, an aerobatic pilot. Little information can be gleaned about pupils who have risen to senior positions in major national organisations, but they are known to include Jane Langdon (The Water Authorities Association) and Brian Beckett (National Consumer Council). Rutland Boughton was the first to have a book written about his life and work. Theodore Zeldin of St. Anthony's College, Oxford must be the most distinguished academic author to have passed through the school if only for his books on French history and his *Intimate History of Humanity (1996)*.

The school has long bred talented musicians. The National Youth Orchestra has drawn recruits from the school on a number of occasions, the first in 1954. Stewart Eaton had the distinction of graduating to the European Community Youth Orchestra in 1977-78. As an outstanding viola player he had experience of the orchestra pit at La Scala before taking the leadership of his section in the London Symphony Orchestra.

Members of the school have enjoyed meeting the distinguished sons of former old boys. There was an exciting visit from the Lord Mayor of London and Lady Gadsden in 1979. It is the custom of the Lord Mayor to visit his old school during his year in office. Sir Peter Gadsden had been educated abroad and chose to visit his father's old school instead. He presented a magnificent cup in memory of the occasion. Shortly afterwards, Gary Mabbutt of the Spurs and England team came with his father to the school fête.

Much of this information has found its way into the national press. Other items of national significance are more easy to obtain because they appear in school records. As league tables began to enter the national scene, the school was naturally anxious about its status. It began by appearing among the top schools in the country for the 'A' level results. A survey in *The Times* of the country's best schools included it in the top hundred. In an *Observer* supplement, it was classified as one of the 66 'Good State Schools in South-East England.' In the OFSTED report of 1995, the school was listed among the 32 best which were inspected during the year, with representatives being invited to a congratulatory reception.

The columns of the national press have likewise been entered by individual pupils. These included the 'young engineer of the year' in 1978. Physics has been very much to the fore. A special prize was awarded by the Institute of Physics to Timothy Henstock for the best 'A' level national entry in 1986. In the British Physics Olympiad, the school had two of the twenty-one gold medals on the first occasion and in 1995, two out of the fifteen. Anthony Stevens made his reputation by scoring the highest marks in mathematics in the Oxford and Cambridge 'A' level examination.

Public speaking, which had been keenly pursued in the school for many years, also claimed attention. It reached a peak in 1992 when the school team was awarded *The Observer Mace*. Subsequently, the team participated in the World Public Speaking Competition in Canada, where a member of the school, Daniel Saxby, was placed second overall. In 1993 the school won the English Speaking Union National Championships with Alex Saxby becoming the individual national champion. At the International Informatics Olympiad in Hungary in 1996, Andrew Cooke represented Great Britain.

National achievements have been similarly recorded in the sporting field, most boys 'graduating' by way of participation in county teams. In 1986, Ian Jones was selected for the British Olympic Fencing Squad. On other occasions, Harley Carter was the county entry for the All England Javelin Championships and Sean Flynn became the England Junior Squash Captain. Andrew Field was British Schools Canoeing Champion in 1987 – by which time boys were building their own canoes in the school's workshop. In the British Schools Tennis Championship, Richard Bones and Jeremy Green won the national event for boys under thirteen. In 1979-80, Mark Rose was selected for the English Schools Rugby side against a number of international teams, and in 1985-86 Patrick Young captained England's Schools under-nineteen XV against an Australian team in Rugby at Twickenham. The following year, the Rugby XV again provided players at the national level. Sometimes there is an unexpected event. An entirely different achievement was the success of the Equestrian Club in the National Schools Cross-Country Championships in 1995, when the team of four became the first boys' school to win this event. So the roll call continues.

Pride rightly exists in all that is being done in the present. It is the purpose of this brief chronicle to trace the steps by which the school has attained the status that it holds today. Perhaps it will also serve to encourage present and forthcoming generations of boys to make the acquaintance of the handsomely restored County Museum (Trench and Fenley, 1993) which housed a very different school for nearly two hundred years. They might even make a pilgrimage to Quarrendon 'a good myle from Aylesberie' (as Leland put it) where, beside the ruins of St. Peter's chapel (in which Sir Henry Lee's mortal remains were buried), English Heritage has placed a plaque identifying the site of his mansion.

In 1850, it was the hope of the leader writer in *The Bucks Advertiser and Aylesbury News* that the Free School might eventually be turned into 'a great Educational Institution' and that, through it, the town might be 'honoured with educational privileges such as it deserves.' Several generations have now contributed to an institution beyond the imaginings of the mid-Victorians, let alone those of Sir Henry Lee and Henry Phillips. It is a happy coincidence that the school, founded in the reign of Elizabeth I, should be celebrating its four hundredth anniversary in the reign of Elizabeth II – and that, additionally, it should be a celebration on the eve of a new millennium.

APPENDIX A

THE ENDOWMENT AT BROUGHTON

The management of the Charity's property at Broughton is best treated separately from the story of the school. It has constituted an item on the agenda of the trustees' meetings from the outset in 1720. The tenancies of the properties were first agreed on September 12, 1722. Thereafter, the accounts balance expenditure and income. Nor was it long before it was realised that there was likely to be considerable expenditure. In 1725, £20 was debited 'for cleansing the mill pond.' In the 1730s repairs to the mill were needed – thatching and tiling, four hundred bricks together with lime and stone, carriage for the timber, a new bridge over the moat. There was a succession of smaller niggling items – land taxes, tithes, ('to ye parson') church rates, poor rates, constable rates, payments for vagabonds, vagrants and quarterages. Some of these were to disappear with the years. The tenants changed fairly frequently. The trustees were apprehensive as to what should be done if a tenant left in debt. They did not have to wait long. One of the Jordan family absconded in 1735. They seized his cattle in lieu of £65 in outstanding rent.

It was necessary to pay a proportion of the costs following the Enclosure Award of Bierton and Hulcott dated July 15, 1780 by 'Act of Parliament made in the nineteenth year of the Reign of the present Majesty King George the Third.' The parcels of land in the open fields were only slowly compacted, but the exercise entailed bills for fencing, planting quickthorns and digging ditches.

Legal issues arose. A small amount of stone was sold from one of the fields ('beer for the stone diggers' was listed under expenditure). In 1808, it was discovered that the local surveyors responsible for road repairs had dug stone in an enclosure of the trustees without permission. Worse still, the gate to the field had been broken down and some

141

Bucks (to wit) *Extracts* from the Award or Instrument bearing date the fifteenth day of July One thousand seven hundred and eighty as inrolled in the Office of the Clerk of the Peace for the County of Bucks pursuant to the Directions of a certain Act of Parliament made in the nineteenth year of the Reign of his present Majesty King George the Third Intitled "An Act for Dividing and Inclosing the open "Common Fields Common Meadows Waste Lands and Commonable Places within the "Parishes and Liberties of Bierton and Hulcott in the County of Bucks"

To the Trustees of certain Lands belonging to Aylesbury Freeschool in lieu of eleven Freehold computed acres with right of Common thereto belonging and also right of Common for two Cottages the two several plots of Land or Ground herein next after described that is to say One plot of Land or Ground lying in Broughton Stoke Lake field containing thirteen acres three roods and

13.3.7

seven perches and in annual value fourteen pounds fifteen shillings and sixpence Farthing Bounded on several parts of the North or North west and East or North East by the said Old Inclosures in Broughton aforesaid called Stoke Lake belonging to Aylesbury Freeschool on part of the South or South East by a public road leading from Broughton to Aylesbury aforesaid on part of the west or South west and on the remaining part of the South or South East by an allotment to the said William Dorey and Henry Geary exchanged with the said Trustees of Aylesbury Freeschool and on the remaining part of the west or south West by an Allotment to the said Earl Nugent Temple And one other plot of land or Ground in the said Millers pen in the said Middle Field of Bierton containing

2.33

two roods and thirty three perches and in annual value eighteen shillings and three pence three Farthing Bounded on the North west by Old Inclosures in Bierton on the North East by an allotment to the said Ralph Earl Verney and on the South East and South west by Old Inclosures in Broughton called + Stoke lake aforesaid The Hedges Ditches and Fences of the said First described Allotment to the said Trustees of Aylesbury School on the south or south East next the said public road

The introduction to the Enclosure Award of July 15, 1780 for Bierton and Hulcott, requiring the School Trustees to enclose the fields allocated to them.

of the stone had been stolen. The surveyors were required to provide compensation. They were also reminded that road metals were only allowed to be carted between April 1 and November 1 and at times of hard frost.

A more serious issue arose as a consequence of the construction of the Aylesbury Branch construction of the Grand Junction Canal which was completed 1814-15. Drainage problems followed and there was interference with springs that fed the mill stream. Samuel Moberley, who had held the tenancy of the mill since 1788, applied to the company for compensation for the loss of water supply. He was unsuccessful, whereupon he took the law into his own hands and cut a channel from the brook that had formerly supplied the Domesday Mill, but now fed the canal. He was immediately indicted for a felony – 'wilfully and maliciously (damaging) the canal to the prejudice of navigation.' Bail was allowed for a sum of £200. The trustees had to sort out the matter. Happily there was a successful conclusion. The Canal Company agreed to pay £1,470 for the right to use the springs and brooks, the Court of Chancery decreeing that the trustees invested the compensation in government stock or real securities.

In 1838, permission was given by Act of Parliament (Gulielmi IV Regis) to the Aylesbury Railway Company for the construction of a link from the town to Cheddington on the London to Birmingham Railway. The price for the compulsory purchase of 2 acres, 3 roods and 23 poles of the Charity's land was agreed by arbitration. The engineer in charge was Robert Stephenson.

A summary of the property held by the Charity was listed in 1832. It consisted of the homestead of Broughton Abbotts embracing a large farmhouse with outbuildings and 141 acres of pastureland; four pieces of pastureland totalling 36 acres, 2 roods, 35 poles; an allotment in Broughton of 2 acres, 33 poles; a corn mill and millhouse with outbuildings and a cottage together with arable and pasture totalling 19 acres, 1 rood and 20 poles. Quit rents were still regularly paid at the time, those paying them including the Duke of Buckingham and Chandos and the Girdlers Company (BRO/CH3/E3). An undated map entitled *A Survey of the Estate at Broughton in the parish of Bierton in Bucks belonging to Aylesbury School* is included among the archives entitled *Aylesbury Free School Property 1852*. The map, with a scale in chains and with a cartouche is probably dated c.1830. It identifies three units of land – Manor Farm and two outlying groups of fields on the other side of the canal. Manor Farm consisted of the Home Ground, the Moor, Court Leys, Cow

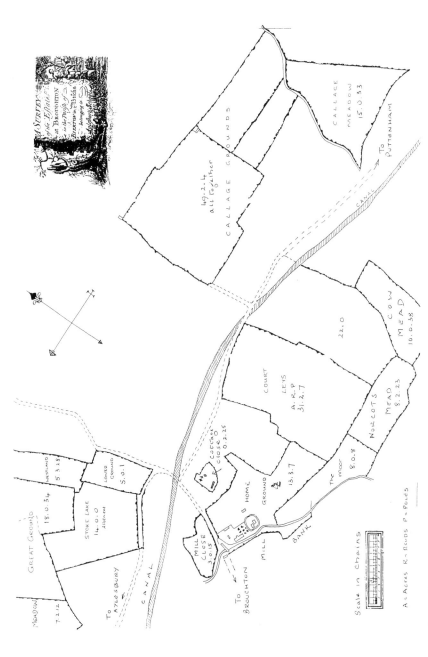

The Cartouche reads 'A survey of the estate at Broughton in the Parish of Bierton in Bucks. Belonging to Aylesbury School'. The map is from about 1830, somewhat faded, with a scale in chains. The Aylesbury Branch of the Grand Junction Canal is a central feature. A 'road to Puttenham' is indicated (it is now a bridle path). There are maps of neighbouring properties in the Buckinghamshire County Record Office.

144

Mead and Norcots Mead. It is bounded on the north by the canal and the 'road to Puttenham' (now a bridle path).

About the same time that the map was drawn the trustees were employing William Bull as a kind of land agent to collect the rents and deal with the tenants. He tried to negotiate on behalf of the trustees the purchase of thirty acres of land in Weston Turville – 'a mile away', but it was frustrated because of a dispute over the ownership (B.R.O./ CH3/E2/25).

The introduction to the Memorandum of Agreement for the Conveyance of Land from the Trustees to the Aylesbury Railway Company, November 12, 1838.

At intervals throughout the nineteenth century, new tenants appear in the Minute Books, though the competition to rent the land declined with the advancing agricultural depression. The demands from the tenants of

145

the mill were perennial. In 1827, an engineer pronounced the mill 'decayed and unfit for repair', yet a new waterwheel was purchased. The stream needed 'sinking' or 'scouring', grazing animals 'trod down its banks', a 'waste water weir' was needed, there were 'deficiencies of water'. In the latter part of the nineteenth century, such were the recurrent problems of the mill bridge and the dilapidations of the associated buildings that there were suggestions that the mill and the head of water should be done away with (30/8/1886). The possibility of selling it, together with the adjacent land, to the existing tenant was raised, but it was felt that the Charity Commissioners would not approve unless 'a very liberal offer' was made (25/10/1886). The bills for maintenance reduced any sympathy that there might have been for the residents of the mill when, having no regular supply of drinking water, they asked to be linked to the pipe of the Chiltern Hills Water Company (11/10/1904). Two years later, the mill stream was sufficiently polluted for a complaint to be received from the Thames Conservancy Board (14/10/1906).

While the school itself advanced on all fronts, the property at Broughton continued to raise problems. In 1937, the school governors were invited to meet members of the Higher Education Sub-committee of the County Council. 'For some years', the committee commented, 'the School Account has made good a deficit on the Foundation Account' – that is, the loss on the Broughton property. The response to the committee was that the endowment had financed the purchase of the land on Walton Road and provided the collateral for the new building in 1907. It was also indicated that the income from the property during the preceding 27 years, after deductions and a small number of annual losses, had produced the sum of £3,472 for school needs. In reply to the suggestion that it might be wise to sell the Broughton property, the governors forecast a loss of both income and capital if such action was taken. There is no denying that Broughton appeared all too often as an unwelcome item on the governors' agenda. During the same decade that the school was enjoying unequalled progress, the modest income from the property was largely swallowed up in maintenance. First came a complaint from the Thames Conservancy Boarrd that a cesspool at Manor Farm was regularly overflowing. It was followed by pressure from the sanitary inspector of the Vale. Next a congested stream caused flooding around the mill. It was necessary to construct a brick dam to control it. Later, a hundred pounds had to be set aside for a pumping unit. Repairs to the bridge, a problem through the generations, continued to drain the finances. A roof needed repairing: a shed collapsed and had to be replaced; dilapidations were reported by tenants. Materials were needed for fencing a meadow. The tenant of Manor Farm pressed for a cottage to be built – a loan for £450 was provided by the Education sub-committee. Land values and farm products suffered from the general depression and a remission of rent was granted to the tenant. At the same time, a rent reduction was requested from the Bierton Parish Council for allotments that were lying uncultivated. A tithe redemption annuity of £11/18/- entered the accounts twice yearly and, interestingly, the 'half moiety of rates'.

The District Council negotiated the purchase of land in Stocklake for the erection of a pumping station to meet the needs of the Bierton sewage system and, on the eve of the war, the school was advised that a proposed 'byepass road' 'would affect Manor Farm at Broughton'. The same little sub-committee of Foundation Governors had to deal with all of these issues. Nor did the outbreak of war eliminate Broughton from the agenda. The War Agriculture Committee required the school's reluctant tenants to plough up their pasture and sow it with grain. In 1943 notice was received of the possible acquisition of most of the Manor Farm land by government contractors, but no further action was taken.

For the decade following the war, only minor problems were recorded in the governors' minutes, but in 1958 concern was expressed about 'the abnormal expenditure on Manor Farm'. It was partly related to repairs to buildings, for which legally the tenant was responsible. 'A substantial contribution' was made to help him, but he was reminded of his obligations. When the new tenancy agreement was negotiated, four groups of farm buildings were treated as beyond repair. A possible improvement grant for the farm house was unsuccessfully investigated.

When the Boys' School came into being, a precise schedule of the Charity's property 'made up to 1 June 1959' was appended to the Ministry of Education paper (March 24, 1960). It is interesting that almost immediately a request was received from the tenant of the Mill

House asking if the Governors would consider selling the property. The Ministry approved the sale of the Mill House without the paddock for £1,500, the paddock to be let at £15 per acre. The proceeds were to be invested in local government stock. Other enquiries were set in motion at the same time. The condition of the Bierton allotments was found to be satisfactory and the lost tenancy agreement (10/3/1961) enquired if the annuity of £23/16/1 could be redeemed. The tithe was payable up to and including the annual instalment due on 1/10/1996. Redemption would cost fifteen times the annual payment and it was decided to take no action.

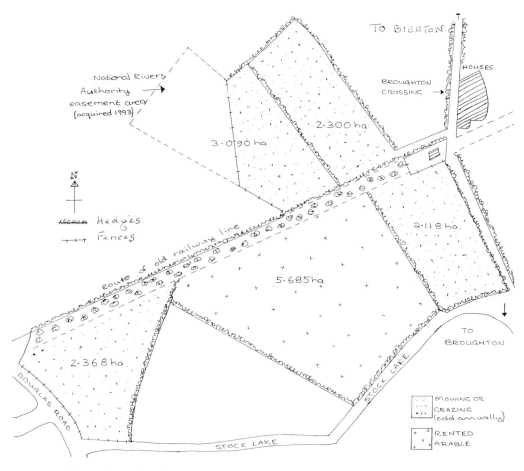

A map of the residue of land retained by the Foundation Governors in Broughton.

Meanwhile, two fields at Stocklake were sold to the District Council at a price agreed by the District Valuer of £26,625. For the school it was a windfall.

The farm house at Manor Farm had become increasingly uninhabitable. Can this be the same timber-framed house that impressed Nicholas Pevsner? (1960 p. 180). In 1964, it was decided that a new four-bedroomed house should be erected in the driveway of the old building on the line of existing services – all subject to the planning approval of the Ministry of Agriculture. It was clearly going to be a prolonged operation and it was suggested that it might be more simple to sell Manor Farm in its entirety. Meanwhile, the tenant would be required to make good in full dilapidations or give up his tenancy partly in lieu. A compromise was reached when he agreed the latter proposal. With vacant possession and the new farm house built, the property was put up for auction. Thus, Manor Farm, the principal component of the old Broughton – cum – Bierton endowment was sold in 1967 for £33,000.

The steady nibbling away of the landed property was to continue. Five fields and a small separate remnant of land are all that remain of the land acquired in 1715 in the possession of the Charity. Three fine fields of meadow hay (8.6 acres, 5.6 acres and 5.3 acres) still display the relic ridge-and-furrow of the open field strips. A third of one of them was acquired in 1992 by the National Rivers Authority for a flood easement scheme. A fourth meadow (6 acres) subject to flooding abuts the Inner Ring Road. A large arable field, for some decades under allotments, has an area of 12.7 acres. The land of the old Aylesbury Junction Railway, purchased in 1838, was returned to the Charity when the line was abandoned. Nigel Furley wrote an account of 'the last ride on the Cheddington Flyer' for *The Aylesburian* in 1953. In her second book of poems, Christine Dunker commemorated 'Marston Gate' halt. Superficially the old track is a valueless thorn scrub. In 1983, the National Rivers Authority also acquired a small parcel of land adjacent to the old mill stream in Broughton, leaving about two acres of grazing land in possession of the Charity.

The rents yielded by the property amount to rather more than £1,000 annually. The *Aylesbury Vale District Plan* (1996) describes the Broughton land as having 'potential for housing and employment.'

APPENDIX B

'A scheme for the management of the Aylesbury Free and Endowed Schools'. July 15 1862

'... the full number of Trustees of the Charity shall be fourteen; and that the Vicar of Aylesbury for the time being and the Incumbent of Walton for the time being shall respectively be two of such Trustees by virtue of their respective Offices, and without any further or other appointment ...

In case of a vacancy or vacancies occurring in the office of Trustees, the remaining Trustees shall appoint a proper person or proper persons to supply such vacancy or vacancies, the person or persons to be appointed being resident within a radius of ten miles from the school-house; such appointments to be forthwith reported to the Charity Commissioners.

For the due administration of the Charity, the Trustees for the time being shall hold four general meetings in every year in the School-house, or at such other place as they shall think fit to appoint, such meetings to be held on such day and at such times as the Trustees shall appoint, and in default of such appointment then such meetings shall be held on the Saturday in the week after the 6th day of April, the Saturday immediately preceding the commencement of the Midsummer Holidays, the Saturday in the week after the 11th day of October and the Saturday immediately preceding the commencement of the Christmas holidays; and that at such meetings the accounts of the School shall be examined, and the conduct and management thereof during the preceding quarter, and the then present state thereof shall be enquired into.

The Trustees shall, at least seven days before the audit, publish in two of the Aylesbury newspapers a summary of the receipts and payments on account of the Charity during the preceding year, together with a notice of the time and place at which it is proposed to audit such accounts.

Boys who have attained the age of seven years, and are able to read, and whose parents are inhabitants of Aylesbury or Walton, or of the next neighbouring parishes (but with a preference in favour of Aylesbury and Walton), and unable of their own means to give them such an education as may be obtained in the Lower School, shall be eligible to become scholars of that School, and that the Head Master shall keep a book wherein he shall enter in rotation the names, ages, and qualifications of all applicants for admission to the Upper and Lower Schools, and shall at every meeting of the Trustees submit such book to them, and they shall have exclusive power at any meeting to admit boys as scholars of either school, and to expel scholars therefrom for irregularity, disobedi- ence, or other improper conduct.

The total number of boys receiving an absolutely gratuitous education upon the foundation shall not exceed 120. That there shall be an Upper and Lower School. That the course of Education in the Lower School shall comprise the English language, writing, arithmetic, book-keeping, accounts, geography, and modern history, and, in addition to the sub- jects taught in the Lower School, the course of education in the Upper shall comprise the Greek, Latin and French languages, mathematics, and such other useful branches of education as the Trustees may from time to time direct. That the free boys in both schools shall be gratuitously supplied and provided with all necessary books, pens, ink, paper, pen- cils, and stationery, and that daily instruction shall be given by the read- ing and explanation of the Holy Scriptures, and the examination of the scholars in their knowledge thereof.

There shall always be one Head Master, who shall be at least a Bachelor of Arts of either of the Universities of Oxford, Cambridge, London, Durham, or Trinity College, Dublin and qualified to teach and instruct the scholars in all the aforesaid branches of education (except writing, arithmetic, book-keeping and accounts), and to supervise the instructions given by the Writing Master in his department, and to judge of the progress of the scholars in all the branches of education taught in the schools, and at least one Second Master, who shall be called the Master of the Lower School, and who shall be qualified to instruct the scholars in all the branches of education taught in the Lower School,, and at least one Writing Master, who shall be qualified to teach the scholars writing, arithmetic, book-keeping, and accounts, and shall perform such other duties as the Head Master shall from time to time appoint.

The Head Master shall be at liberty to appoint one or more Assistant Master or Masters, to be approved by the Trustees, but not to be considered as having any vested interest under this scheme.

All boys attending the Upper School shall pay a capitation fee not exceeding one guinea and half per quarter if residing with their parents or guardians in Aylesbury or Walton, if residing elsewhere two guineas per quarter, except that a number of boys, not less than ten, may, after one year's regular attendance at the Lower School, be elected by the Trustees to Exhibitions admitting them free to the Upper School. That expensive books such as Lexicons, Atlases etc., may be provided by the Trustees, and that each boy in the Upper School, except the free boys, pay 2s 6d per quarter for the use of them. Stationery and ordinary school books required by the pay boys in the Upper School to be provided by such boys.

The capitation fees and payments mentioned in the last clause be paid in advance quarterly to the Head Master and accounted for by him to the Trustees, to be applied by them to the improvement of the income of the Head Master, the maintenance of an Assistant Master or Masters in either of the said schools, and to such other purposes as the Trustees shall from time to time appoint, provided only that the present Head Master shall receive not less than one half of such capitation fees.

There shall be paid to the Head Master, the Master of the Lower School, and the Writing Master, such annual salaries as the Trustees, having regard to the resources of the Charity, shall from time to time determine; and the Head Master and the Lower Master shall be respectively entitled to, and shall be paid in addition to their said several salaries, the sums or allowances following, (that is to say) the Head Master at the rate of ten shillings per annum, and the Lower Master at the rate of five shillings per annum, in respect of each boy, not exceeding in number 120, who shall have been admitted into either school upon the foundation, and shall have *bona fide* attended school during the preceding quarter, and such salaries and payments to be made quarterly.

The present Head Master and the Lower Master shall be entitled, free of rent, to, and shall if required by the Trustees, reside in the residences belonging to the Charity now occupied by them respectively.

Subject to the controlling power of the Trustees, the Head Master shall have the entire Government of both schools, and that the Lower and other Masters shall perform such duties as he shall from time to time direct.

The expense of providing fuel to be used in the schools and of cleaning the school-rooms shall be paid and borne out of the income of the Charity.

The Head Master shall be at liberty to receive any number of boys as boarders in his house, not exceeding twenty, to be instructed with the other boys in the Upper School, but subject to the payment to the trustees of the capitation fees hereinbefore mentioned.

Neither of the Masters shall (except as in these Statutes mentioned), in respect of their teaching of any of the scholars, receive from any of them or any of their parents or friends any payment, gift or present whatsoever, without the sanction of the Trustees.

The only holidays in the schools shall be the days between the Thursday before and the Wednesday next after Easter Day, Monday and Tuesday in Whitsun week and one month at Midsummer, and one month at Christmas, and the afternoon of every Wednesday and Saturday throughout the year.

The Head Master shall keep a separate list of the boys admitted to each school, which shall state the date of the admissions the names and ages of the boys, the names and residences of their parents or guardians, and the dates and reasons of their leaving the school; and that the Head Master shall have power to suspend until the next meeting of the Trustees any scholar who shall be guilty of irregularity, disobedience, or other improper conduct in either school.

That an examination by a competent person or persons, to be nominated by the Trustees, of all the scholars for the time being in the schools, as to their proficiency, shall be held immediately preceding the Midsummer holidays and the Christmas holidays, and that the inhabitants of Aylesbury and Walton shall be at liberty to attend such examinations; and that the Trustees shall have power to award such and so many prizes, not exceeding twenty in number, as they may think fit, to and amongst the most meritorious scholars of either school, who shall distinguish themselves for learning or good conduct, and who in the judgement of the examiners shall be deserving of the same, provided that the total amount to be expended in the purchase of such prizes at any one examination shall not exceed the sum of £10, and no greater sum than £10 shall be paid to any examiner or examiners for any one examination, unless with consent of the Charity commissioners.

This scheme shall be printed at the expense of the Charity, and a copy thereof given to every person who is now or may hereafter be appointed a Trustee or Master of or in the schools, and a copy thereof shall be supplied by the Head Master to any person who shall be willing to pay the sum of one shilling for the same.'

There are other rules – details relating to the conducting of the affairs of the Charity and estates, but they do not affect the general management of the schools.

The Head Boys and Heads of the Six Houses 1997–98

Back Row (from left to right)
Chris Crabtree, Simon Kiff, Patrick Dean, Ben Wilkinson
Front Row (from left to right)
Neill Pearman, Matthew Warren, Sam Cottman, Nick Smart, Clive Rhodes.

APPENDIX C

Pupils by Tutor Group - As at 25 September 1997

YEAR 14

M J Berry
M P Goodman
C Lang

DENSON 13

W R Arkell
S P Axtell
T P Bailey
M R Bernstein
P B Bradley
D S Bundock
C J Crabtree
A M Dalton
S M Evans
T J Fraser
C P Gordon
P W Grater
N J Higgins
F J Holland
O R Hook
D M Hulse
I Jalloh
A J John
A J Killip
R J King
E W Lydall
B G Pammenter
A D Parkhurst
M C Parks
P S Poinen
G W Rose
C S Royle
M S Suleman
A R Todd
S J Trigg

J A Wallis
M N Warren

HAMPDEN 13

I A Ashbridge
S J Benbow
D J Bleach
D A Brown
J R Carey
B A Cleland
R A Cooper
A P Cotterill
S M Cottman
J F Cumberland
J A Dagley
L J Davies
I Defriez
A G Dix
L J Elmore
O J Hall
J C Hankers
B W Huxley
H T Jardine
A Kapadia
O A Kiani
S J Kiff
S P Mccloskey
M Mcloughlin
P J Merrell
S Page
A R Piers
T G Price
A J Roche
C F Stovold
A K Surendran
U Ul-Haq

G S Vale

LEE 13

L Bartlett
S C Bland
J T Boorman
C M Brandon
A J Cogger
R E Crockford
H O Fraser
R Friggieri
M W Grace
M E Hadfield
A G Hale
M C Hill
M O Hollings
J Insley
R Kirkham
K S Meek
D C Merriman
S A Newcombe
A M Nuckley
J P O'flynn
C M Payne
T M Pringle
M J Sadler
J M Seward
K M Steel
E L Sweeney
O D Taylor
N Vadia
B Wilkinson
C R Williams
T A Wright

PATERSON 13

T D Ashton
M A Bailey
R S Barrett
G P Bennison
J M Borchard
N J Bowden
T D Brooker
K J Bush
G M Cotton
S P Dixon
A J Gibson
P D Giles
S Q Griffin
P Hodgkinson
G T Hoskins
D K How
O G Moore
R W Muirhead
A M Nicholas
S Nuseibeh
D B Owens
D C Padbury
B S Pickard
S N Prebble
A Rehman
C W Rhodes
K Taylor
O G Tebbutt
A J Walker
J W Woodfield
R M Woollford
R Young

PHILLIPS 13

S J Barclay
T Basu
S D Beazley
D Biggs
A J Bond
A J Bourbon
T D Bowers
R J Buck
G P Clark
N J Collins
P M Dean

J E Fleet
A J Goates
A D Hird
C K Lane
S Malduca
G A Moody
D S Olliffe
N J Osborn
A D Page
G J Palmer
A M Piddington
H Rashid
N G Salter
N L Smart
N A Spicer
B Ward
N J Wrenn
H J Young

RIDLEY 13

W S Arrowsmith
J R Bailey
G Bell
J A Berry
M W Brown
J Buckley
T J Chandler
M A Crowe
S G Direkze
J A Godfrey
D M Greaves
T J Holden
B J Holkham
A R Holroyd
J J Horn
A Houldsworth
D P Johnstone
A J Lea
G B Lewis
B M Luckman
J K Marshall
K J Mcaleavey
J D Mooney
D A Murphy
L B Parker
N J Pearman

B G Pearson
D F Perowne
C E Phillips
A K Russell
S P Sharp
A J Walsh
G R Williams
M G Williams

DENSON 12

S R Adams
J Anderson
P D Brimicombe
M J Brown
A Cornish
J E Craker
H C Darley
C Devlin
L T Downes
A J Duthie
A M Fraser
M Fraser
A D Gold
G Hall
J M Jackson
E H Jefferson
P A Knox
J Mistry
A Mohiuddin
P J Molloy
A R Mylles
S J Newson
M Patel
R A Penrose
T J Phillips
J A Richardson
N M Rickus
M A Scheu
G D Slee
P W Tang
W Vazquez
I R Westgate
T J Wilson
D P Wood

HAMPDEN 12

P Ashford
W E Britton
E J Cadwallader
R G Cameron-Mowat
J Cooper
N W Davies
P Eacott
J M Evans
M J Evershed
S J Goodright
H S Hothi
D P Jones
P D Kennedy
A Linehan
S J Mclellan
J P Miller
L R Parr
S Patel
T M Rawlings
S P Rogers
G J Shepherd
G M Shrubsole
S M Storey
A J Sweetman
N Tahsin
C Tautz
A J Tovey
D M Wale
A N Warnock-Smith
P D Whitehouse
S Wilson
M C Wright
S York

LEE 12

D S Barrance
M Beckett
K Brogan
R C Budd
J C Carroll
C J Dawson
O J Dawson
P Djuric
S P Foster
P Houghton

A J Hutson
G S Jones
I A Khan
S Martin
B J Merrett
N J Metherell
C Morris
D Mould
R J Mynard
I T Paterson
D E Pearce
A L Raven
K S Read
C T Ross
J L Shield
G C Sweetman
B Taylor
D L Todd
M J Wallace
D Ward
K R Wastell
A J Webster
R L Wiffin
B S Wilson
M J Young

PATERSON 12

S L Barnes
J D Bowe
W Broadribb
L R Brooker
W Burns
B M Currie
P H Davis
A J Ellis
M T Elwin
M R Harlock
M R Hay
T S Johnson
J Lapham
J A Lewton
E G Mccairns
I A Miller
I Mohammad
R A Murphy
T J O'halleran

C J Partner
J P Pennicott
D J Purser
C Puttick
O S Roberts
D J Seymour
R Shah
J A Skinner
R T Smith
S J Smith
P K Spencer
K A White
A J Wright
C J Yates

PHILLIPS 12

C P Argles
M G Barlow
A K Bhattacharyya
M J Binder
P W Brabin
M J Buck
S D Burke
W F Clarke
P H Crookall
C Doneth-Hillier
M Dudley
O O Ejikeme
O L Grouille
R J Hall
N E Hallatt
R G Hamilton
S Hanrahan
C H Laferton
A J Lowndes-Knight
C D Miskin
C J Priest
R L Prior
M Riches
A E Richmond
N J Roach
D A Scutt
V M Selvarajah
H E Simpson
S M Thomas
K J Walsh

R Westbrooke
S T Whiffin
R J Wiltshire
D J Woodcock
S Zaman

RIDLEY 12

A P Aminian
D J Andrews
M T Baker
R M Beales
J D Bellin
J S Corn
G M Deli
R Dorman
M P Ellington
J Frost
R J Giles
S B Godagama
R O Goodwin
J G Higginson
M J Kilpatrick
P V Kindell
A D Mcnicol
M B Middleton
R S Middleton
D Pang
A E Paterson
M A Phillips
W Rehman
P M Rowe
R J Scott
A M Simms
S J Sylvester
E J Tyrrell
M G Vallis
C J Wells
A J Wilson

DENSON 11

J C Ainley
R J Baxter
T C Bird
R J Brockett
H K Callychurn
M T Curry

C G Davidson
T N Edwards
A W Ferris
R A Friday
D R Grayson
A J Henney
J R Holland
D P Hook
K E Kaye
D R Kennedy
H R Miles
P J Mitchell
G O Morgan
O J Newing
T Oakman
T M Pammenter
D A Phillips
L J Pitcher
N I Rose
J P Royle
N Ryan
J P Sheard
M A Smith
C T Winterbottom

HAMPDEN 11

T B Akindoyin
D P Baker
A M Banville
S A Benskin
M Bowden
C A Boylan
A H Cameron-Mowat
J D Cleland
S D Cook
I J Deay
A J Durrans
R J Foster
J M Fowler
J M Fulton
O S Gillinson
B A Hall
R M Hodnett
K C Hudson
O J Jackson
C T Jansen

A J Jones
C D Knowles
G L Manning
D J Mills
A J Munday
J P Partington
A J Pitkin
J S Smith
N S Stovold
R C Thursby
D R Wilson
D J Woodfield

LEE 11

R A Allen
C T Baker
G F Brooks
K A Budd
D J Carr
D A Crump
J R Dlugosz
A J Donnan
A P Dove
J D Grant
M J Griffiths
M C Hadfield
M J Harrison
M R Hemming
K J Hewer
S J Holland
M A Kadom
J M Langlands
C M Merrylees
N J Mitchell
G Morris
A M Paterson
S J Rackley
J R Rainford
S S Sangha
J G Stone
M J Stubberfield
P A Toler
B C Tomes
J D West
L Wilkinson
M J Wragg

PATERSON 11

N E Adams
M M Ageli
R J Bartlett
R P Boudour
G Burns
J A Campbell
J E Carr-Barnsley
T M Falk
W J Gatherer
P D Gaulton
D C Hallsworth
L C Holden
T L Holton
G E Jones
M K Jones
S A Karia
G J Martindale
A P Mudditt
V Patel
M C Pearce
P G Richmond
P R Savage
J R Senior
R A Smith
I J Spencer
N Srinivasan
G Stanley
B M Suter
H S Thomas
M J Williams
A F Woolf

PHILLIPS 11

J P Austin
J R Booth
P E Brant
P J Brown
J E Butler
J L Card
K J Carruthers
A J Conway
R O Denham
S G Eccles
M A Evans
D W Fleming

B Francis
R E Ghosh
J M Hird
S P Holmes
A C Jones
A D Lowndes-Knight
S Morris
D Osborne
R J Paterson
O I Poole
C Ratcliff
D J Read
J D Scadden
E M Sheerin
F J Simonds
J P Smith
A C Stone
D J Vella
C A Wiltshire

RIDLEY 11

N R Adams
P W Albrighton
R C Arrowsmith
J D Atkins
C J Bailey
J D Boyd-Kirkup
C S Chandler
E J Croker
T H Fairfield
R D Foy
H C Goodwin
S Hamilton
D J Hewitt
R K Holkham
R M Jeffery
R G Johnstone
O J Kelley
A R Kemp
G J Mander
J E Marshall
P R Murphy
J W Pearce
A H Preston
J M Rae
P M Sheppard

A G Stevens
C R Tranfield
E G Turner
J J Wallington
C A Whiles
N R Woodhouse
J C Wright

DENSON 10

S W Armstrong
D S Belam
S J Benjamin
W R Dales
G G Downes
M J Duffy
M J Goodall
O E Henderson
A Heng
J P Hood
J Kapadia
S Kusre
T C Lane
J F Loader
L A Loftas
T P Loundon
D J Mace
G R Martin Hall
R J Middleton
J F Newson
B M Passaro
R Patel
W D Rumsey
A J Scott
M A Strain
D J Styles
R D Tamone
R A Watson
G A Watts

HAMPDEN 10

R I Andrew
J W Baker
B J Bingham
J Calvert
M J Calvert
M Colyer

D L Ennis
G N Garnade
J R Hardern
G A Joyner
S L Kennedy
L R Layfield
A J Mcgowan
A G Mcmeekin
P J Mullins
A C Nicholson
J R Osbaldeston
S J Parsons
C D Ramsay
I R Rowett
A J Scott
A E Suppiah
N H Suppiah
M Tanweer
S C Thomas
T R Tilley
J A Tucker
S L Turner
P A Wright

Lee 10

T M August
T Bailey
A Blackburn
B W Carr
G M Casey
J Chan
B R Crompton
M Evans
R G Floutier
R A Freeman
D J Gibbons
M S Gill
S Green
A M Gubler
D R Hares
C N Howard
D P James
K Knight
J E Lawler
H H Lossock
S A Merriman

C Moran
M S Pearce
M J Rawlins
D J Ross
A S Russell
K Wadhwa
M D Wells

Paterson 10

I M Baker
C J Belgrove
W T Bowe
J R Brydon
L Chan
P K Christian
H K Chu
R M Dodds
M N Guina
M T Hillsdon
A W Howard
N D Johnson
F G Jones
L T Jones
R J Leivers
C R Lodge
A J Mchardy
G B Milton
C L Ore
J C Ore
A E Pusey
A S Robinson
J M Shields
T G Short
H L Sutcliffe
C D Taylor
T Thangarajah
W M Thomas
B M Thompson
C Zenkner

Phillips 10

G W Abbott
R Austen-Smith
M J Burke
N A Cooper
J W Dallow

M E Dudley
D J Feore
M A Gray
D J Hamilton
B J Hammett
M B Kerr
O J Lake
R A Lee
T R Moran
C R Nicholas
J G Page
J D Roach
S C Roest
S F Rolfe
A R Selvarajah
A J Shilton
A A Smith
M C Southall
J Sutton
J M Taylor
M J Tully
L A Weatherhead
P J Webster
I Zaman

Ridley 10

P S Ackroyd
M D Baker
A P Cleveland
M J Coll
S J Crompton
D Ditoro
J A Eden
M T Griffin
R G Heeley
M J Hodges
D Jeffery
B D Kempster
S H Kilpatrick
D J Maris
T A Mooney
W A Moore
L O'Sullivan
A J Pleeth
R A Prestidge
R W Pritchard

R S Rogers
I W Rolfe
P J Snell
P B Stennings
J Tang
C D Thomas
P A Wallis
T L Weisner
C R Williams

DENSON 9

M J Adam
G Auld
C E Bates
L O Budka
B D Clay
G C Davenport
R J Doak
T E Evans
D J Fazakerley
A P Goodin
D P Green
D J Harris
A W Hoggart
D L Kaye
M P Kennedy
J A Macisaac
R R Malpas
T N Marsden
A L Mclennan
S C Needs
A O Price
C M Punch
M A Robinson
L J Skinner
M P Varey
C A Vinson
S A Whittington
M T Winterbottom
N R Wood

HAMPDEN 9

G C Ash
B Athi
D R Boniwell
J C Bown

G N Butler
M R Deay
P B Dix
J G Evans
T W Hall
P J Harris
A D Hodgkinson
J V Kendall
A J Logsdail
M Marston
M Mclellan
J C Morton
E Ohashi
J M Pim
M C Prosser
G Ramdyal
K E Randall
J P Reynier
G J Rickard
G C Sirisena
L C Smith
J Spurway
M J Thorpe
J A Wells
I S Wilson
D A Worthington

LEE 9

C J Bianca
M J Brand
R O Brown
M E Burton
P S Cooper
M M Edwards
J P Ellis
P J Esson
S T Friggieri
C P Gordon
P S Grace
C S Hannon
R J Hay
A J Hughes
C M Hunter
S J Jackman
S K Kirkwood
C K Lawton

M T Manning
D J Seward
A N Shute
O P Stanyer
H M Sweeney
D Taylor
D C Templeton
N J Verron
J P Walmsley
A J Watkins
N M West
T J Willdridge
M Williams
D S Williamson

PATERSON 9

J M Birbeck
J R Bowden
J P Brown
P J Cahill
T W Cann
C J Collins
M O Dannhauser
J Evans
D J Fanning
A J Higgons
M J Hiscock
T A Hodges
D P Hunter
M D Jones
C A Judd
M A Legge
R M Leggett
R I Marsh
K R Masters
S R Michell
G W Mullins
K Patel
N V Pavan
C M Pires
D R Prebble
Y S Puwar
A S Shaw
G A Tebbutt
M P Thomas
A Wreglesworth

PHILLIPS 9

M W Abbott
S P Beales
M J Bonne
P E Browne
A D Burrows
O D Chantler
P M Chapman
J W Clark
N L Copcutt
C J Cunningham
C R Evans
A Faulkner
K J Gordon
T A Gregory
D S Hall
T P Hussey
R F Jenkins
M T Jones
I E Lock
S Mehta
D R Porthouse
K Ray
J R Reddington
D M Scullion
M J Scullion
C D Smith
A P Tidmarsh
A R Vijayaratnam
M J Ward
N J Webster
K W Young

RIDLEY 9

D L Baker
L P Banfield
W J Bidder
C I Burgess
A J Byng
K N Charik
R M Croker
J A Cross
S D'angelo
D J Damarell
C J Emerson
M E Evans

A D Fox
S Hosseini-Gerami
N W John
N C Jones
M N Keates
M P King
J J Lynch
S M Lyon
R S Patterson
M R Pearce
T E Peters
B R Porter
A J Pritchard
A Rixon
J M Roper
R P Russell
C W Selby
A J Sneddon
R I Taylor
P J Wilkinson

DENSON 8

A W Back
R T Baker
E G Beardshaw
C P Biggs
M G Blaikie
M G Brabin
S P Bradley
A J Brewer
W R Bridges
N A Bulpett
A Clarkson
C R Clarkson
D R Curtis
B D Galloni
R A Hook
M C Howard
B G Lamb
B Liu
P T Mitchell
J R Orchard
A F Passaro
R J Price
D K Renaud
P J Smith

T D Sturley
E J Tang
C J Williams
H H Wong
D J Wynne-Jones
K Yeung

HAMPDEN 8

O L Armitstead
M A Backler
L J Baker
D J Brennan
E J Britton
A P Conacher
M P Donohoe
T A Fowler
L A Garnade
D H Gillis
J A Griffin
G A Haselgrove
A M Hocking
R O Hunt
T R Layfield
S Leese
H Luchmun
D A Lyons
A D Marshall
R I Marston
P J Nicholls
A P Norton
N J Owen
R J Powell
J E Price
M Silvey
J T Smillie
A P Summerfield
M C Walker
D J Wathen
I D Watters

LEE 8

M S Aldis
N J Andrews
A J Barrett-Mold
T D Beasley
C G Bulpett

P O Carleton
S J Chew
A T Choy
R E Cragg
C Cumming
N J Dablin
M D Evans
A J Fairfield
A N Fernandez
D O Gallagher
C J George
T W Gibby
C P Hamblin
A G Harrison
J W Henderson
J J Hennessy
R J Hill
A J Longton
M Mansour Hughes
D J Merrett
D A Payne
P C Rice
F J Skillen
R J Taylor
C R Tomlinson
S J Wood

PATERSON 8

A J Beckett
R M Bennett
T Bennett
M Bennison
D C Christian
A D Collings
R A Devas
J R Donald
E J Draper
A J Evans
P D Fellows
A J Hallsworth
D A Higgons
E R Horn
A P James
J W Jewell
B M Jiggins
M A Johnson

T E Knight
S C Lockwood
M V Mcdaid
C P Mulcaster
D J Sage
M D Spence
T P Taptiklis
B M Waddams
D J Wainwright
R S Wilson
A H Witt
B J Zealley

PHILLIPS 8

B S Baker
K M Beesley
G P Bonne
J D Brant
R W Bush
C J Calcroft
J R Collins
O Ellis
K R Erlandsen
T J Farmer
A I Flexer
C J Fuchter
S M Hodges
D M Ireland
D E Knight
R F Laferton
T H Lake
T J Lampit
H Mahmood
D J Martin
M J O'sullivan
N R Roe
P D Rogan
G W Ross
A W Rothwell
J E Sutton
N R Talbot
B A Underwood
M C Westerman
J S Williams
A Zaman

RIDLEY 8

N J Angood
J W Barclay
A J Blowing
P T Chandler
O J Coll
T M Cox
J R Curtis
M R Das
D A De Silva
A J Dean
C J Galley
L P Hodges
O G Kuhn
D C Leach
S Mace
K N Mancz
L P Mark
D L McCann
A D McGill
N M Parker
N J Peters
J M Rae
J L Render
S J Roper
M J Ruxton
J Silbermann
D M Sipple
I J Snell
P W Sylvester
K A Tyrrell
J M Willis

APPENDIX D

Foundation Governors	Mr. J.M.A. Paterson, O.B.E (Chairman)
	Professor W.R. Mead
	Dame Kathleen Raven, D.B.E.
	Mr. G. Warrington
L.E.A. Governors	Mrs. G.M.M. Miscampbell, O.B.E
	J. Wilding
	J.A. Prodger
	Mrs. B. Jennings
Co-opted Governors	Mrs. J. Dennis
Teacher Governors	Mrs. D.E. Davies
	Dr D.G. Orchard
Parent Governors	Mr. K. Hardern
	Mrs. M. Kendall
	Mr. G. Lewis
	Mrs. C. Shields
Headmaster	I.P. Roe

APPENDIX E

A NOTE ON STAFF AT THE SCHOOL 1678-1900

This is a very provisional statement. It should be possible to compile a virtually complete list by examining minutely and cross-checking the information in the Account Books and Minute Books from 1720. The Account Books list payments to staff (not always very precisely) and the Minute Books do not consistently record appointments and retirements. All of the early masters of the school were either vicars or curates of Aylesbury Church.

1678	The Rev. Obadiah Dumea	
1680	The Rev. John Higgins	From R. Gibbs, *History of Aylesbury*
1681	The Rev. John Hine	(1870. p. 477)
1687	The Rev. Ralph Gladman	
	Subsequently Master of the New School	
1725	In post The Rev. William Mason, Master of the Latin School	
	Francis North, Writing Master	
	John Boughton, Usher	
1727	The Rev. William Pugh, Master of the Latin School	
	James Neale, Writing Master	
1744	The Rev. John Stephens, Master of the Latin School	
	Robert Neale, Writing Master (son of James and formerly usher)	
	Francis Neale, Usher	
1774	The Rev. William Stockins, Master of the Latin School	
	John Hilliard, Writing Master, formerly Usher	
	William Hickman, Usher	
1783	William Freeman, Usher	
1791	Joseph Wynne, Second Usher	
1797	Thomas de Fraine, Writing Master	
1806	The Rev. John Rawbone succeeds The Rev. William Stockins	

1813 Reappointment of The Rev. William Stockins
1817 The Rev. Charles Robert Ashfield, Master
      Henry Heyward, Writing Master (there is a photograph of him in the school archive c. 1850)
1821 Mr. John Bettsworth, Usher
1829 The Rev. Benjamin Robert Perkins, Master
1834 Mr. J.F. Seymour
1837 The Rev. John Grant Lawford, Master
1840 The Rev. Frederick Cox, Master
1852 Staff consisted of The Rev. Cox, Messrs. Berker, Casler, and Hayward
1862 In post The Rev. Alfred William Howell
1889 Staff consisted of The Rev. A. Howell, The Rev. E. Ridley and Mr. W. Casler
1893 The Rev. Christopher Ridley, Headmaster
1895 Thomas Osborne, Assistant. First Headmaster of New School
1903 Walter Cranley, Writing Master
1897 J.R. Smith, Assistant

The trustees elected 1714–1838 are listed in Lipscomb (p. 64)

APPENDIX F

STAFF AT THE SCHOOL Academic Year 1997–98

Headmaster: I.P. Roe, B.A. (Leics)
Deputy Headmasters: R.G. Kemp, M.A. (Oxon)
C.J. Williams, B.A. (Lond)

C.J. Armitstead, B.A. (Cantab)
J.M. Barrie, B.A. (Liverpool)
Mrs. V. Bates, B.A. (Wolverhampton)
S.J. Bird, B.A. (N.Stafford)
Dr. C.A. Blyth, B.A. & D.Phil. (Oxon)
K.R. Bond, B.Sc. (Lond), Ph.D. (Exeter)
Mrs. J.C. Brimicombe, M.A. (Oxon)
Mrs. J. Brooker, B.A. (Ulster)
Mrs. E.L. Cannon, B.A. (Wales)
P.E. Chesworth, B.A. (Southampton)
J.S. Clarke, B.A. (Loughborough)
Mrs. P.A. Cobb, B.Mus.(Cardiff) B.Phil. (Birm)
B.C. Collyer, M.A. (Cantab)
T.J. Crapper, M.A. (Oxon)
Mrs. S.J. Crowle, B.Sc. (Dunelm)
Mrs. D.E. Davies, B.Ed. (Bristol)
P.N. Dean, B.Ed. (Liverpool)
Mrs. J.M. Deay, B.Sc. (Umist)
C.D. Draper, M.A. (Cantab)
M.J. Edwards, B.Sc. (Lond)
P.W. Elliott, B.Sc. (Dunelm)
J.W. Ferris, B.A. (Trinity College, Dublin)
Mrs. P.M. Fiske, B.Sc. (Exeter)
Mrs. K.M. Ford, B.A. (Sheff)
Mrs. V.A. Francis, B.A. (Herts)
J.E. Furse, B.Mus. (Lond)
S.F. Good, B.A. (Open)
Mrs. G.F. Granger, B.Ed. (Man)
A.R. Grant, J.P., B.A. (Kent At Canterbury)

R.J. Grayson, D.Phil. (Oxon)
P.E. Green, B.Sc. (Man), M.A. (Lond)
Mrs. P.A. Hallatt, B.Sc. (Lond)
B.P. Hancock, B.Ed. (N.E. Wales Institute)
I.R. Hancock, B.Sc. (Lond)
T. Hancock, M.A. (Cantab)
J.S. Harford, B.Sc. (Notts)
Mrs. C. Jiggins, B.Sc. (Lond)
D.W. Jones, M.A. (Oxon)
P.J. Larkham, M.A. (Oxon)
A.R. Lloyd, B.Ed (Plymouth)
Mrs. D.J. Lydall, B.A. (Essex)
A.D. Mcintosh, Ph.D (Edinburgh)
C.R. Mead, B.A. (Lond)
M. Middleton, B.Sc. (Leics)
C.D. Milsom, B.A. (Lond)
Mrs. A.J. Montague, B.A. (Kent)
Mrs. S. Motteram, B.A. (Lond)
C.G. O'Donovan, B.Sc., (Lond), M.A. (Open)
D.G. Orchard, B.Sc., Ph.D. (Sheffield)
A.J. Ormanroyd, M.A. (Cantab & Alberta)
Mrs. J.K. Pearson, B.A. (Newport)
D. Piggford, B.A. (Dunelm)
A.D. Price, B.A. (York)
G.J. Ramsbottom, B.A. (Cardiff)
C.E. Roberts, B.A. (Newcastle)
A.M. Robson, B.A. (Newcastle)
C.N. Rodgers, B.Sc., Ph.D. (Leics & Birm)
C.J. Sage, B.A. (Sheffield)
Mrs. G. E. Allen

The School Staff 1997–98

173

M. W. Thompson
Mrs. S. Thorogood
Mrs. H. A. Williams
Mrs. C.L. Yarrow
P. Carpenter
I. F. Cornish
D. H. Dixon
R.A. Sargeant
A.M. Sessa, B.A. (Colgate), B.D. (Uts N.York)
K.J. Smith, B.Sc., Ph.D (Southampton)

C.M. Sugg, M.A. (Oxon)
Mrs. E.L. Tate, B.A. (Hull)
Mrs. A. Thomas, L De L (Paris)
S.H. Thornley, B.Ed. (Greenwich)
Mrs. P. Venning, B.A. (Lond)
R.J. Warner, B.A. (Warwick)
G.K. Williams, B.Eng. (Liverpool)
Miss R.M. Williams, B.A. (Cardiff)
Miss J.A. Williamson, B.A. (Oxon)
S. Winman, B.Ed. (Exeter)
Mrs. G.H. Wotton, B.Sc. (Bristol)

Support Staff

Mrs. J. Arnold
Mrs. L. M. Bomken
Mrs. M. T. Booth
Mrs. J. L. Brown
Mrs. L. Bomken
M. R. Fraser
M. E. Fyles
Mrs. V. J. Galatin
C. M. Giddings
Mrs. S. M. Giddings
Mrs. M. K. F. Goudge
Mrs. M. A. Green

Mrs. L. Hancock
J. C. Harcourt
Mrs. V. Kennedy
Mrs. C. S. Martin
Mrs. H. G. Murray
Mrs. P. Noble
Mrs. A. D. O'connor
Mrs. E. Ormanroyd
Mrs. J. M. Reeks
Mrs. M. R. Rutland
Mrs. S. E. Steeden
J. K. Tarry

APPENDIX G

A NOTE ON SOURCES

The County Record Office (its archives classified nationally as BRO) houses the principal archives of the Charity School.

CH3/M 1–10	Minute Books of the Trustees/Governors 1720–1952
CH3/AG 1–7	General Administration
CH3/AC 1–16	General Correspondence 1929–46
CH3/E 1–15	Estate Papers 1715–1958
CH3/FAI 1–23	Accounts
CH3/FA2	Accounts of Receipts and Disbursements 1725–47
CH3/G 1–2	Government of the school 1862–1903
CH3/L1	Legal Papers 1850–1860
AG11/89/18	Aylesbury Grammar School Minutes of Governors' Meetings 1952–67

On deposit 1968–88

DX/516	Papers of Alfred C. Young (1893–1975)

There are miscellaneous documents in the safe keeping of the Charity's solicitors, Messrs. Horwood and James. These include the minutes of the Foundation Governors' meetings.

The School Archive contains:

1. Admissions Registers for the Upper and Lower School – 1844–1902, 1851–1881, 1851–1886, 1862–1905, 1862–1907. There is a separate register 1905–1912.

2. A List of Prizewinners 1862–1924. (No prizes were given during the First World War).

3. Staff Registers 1903–1952.

4. Governors' Book 1907–1938, containing brief reports by governors on their inspections.

5. There are school dinner registers, syllabus books, a miscellany of old examination papers and account books and sundry exercise books donated by former pupils (especially those of Mrs. Doris Tompkins). There is also a file compiled by Mrs. Jean Belger of newspaper clippings and correspondence from parents and others covering the threatened comprehensivisation.

The Aylesburian 1908–1914, 1920–1922, 1927–1939, 1946 to date.

The Bucks Advertiser and Aylesbury News (founded 1836).

The Bucks Herald (founded 1832).

The Old Aylesburian Association Newsletter (ed. Joy Waters 1969 to date).

BIBLIOGRAPHY

Ashfield, L.J. and Haworth, C.M., *The History of the Royal Grammar School, High Wycombe,* High Wycombe 1962

Bickersteth, Edward, The Chapel of St. Peter *Records of Bucks,* 2, 22–27, 1863

Broad, John (ed), *Buckinghamshire Dissent and Parish Life, 1660–1712 Buckinghamshire Record Society,* 23, MCMXCIII

Carlisle, Nicholas, *A concise list of the Grammar Schools of England and Wales,* London, 1818

Chambers, E.K., *Sir Henry Lee, an Elizabethan Portrait,* Oxford, 1966

Dale, C.T., *Liverymen of London in 1700* (Guildhall Library)

David, R.W. *Political change and continuity, 1760–1885, a Buckinghamshire Study,* Newton Abbot, 1972

Dictionary of National Biography, Vol. 32, 1892, 356–7

Gibbs, Robert, *Natives of Buckinghamshire and Men of Note in the County,* Aylesbury, 1855

Gibbs, Robert, *A History of Aylesbury,* Aylesbury, 1870

Hanley, Hugh, *The Prebendal, Aylesbury, A History,* 1986

Manuscripts of the Most Hon. The Marquess of Salisbury, London, 1883

Hurd, Michael, *Rutland Boughton and the Glastonbury Festivals,* Oxford 1993

Lipscomb, George, *A History and Antiquities of the County of Buckinghamshire,* 1847, Vols. I–IV, especially Vol. II

Mead, W.R., *Aylesbury, a Personal Memoir from the 1920s,* Aylesbury 1994

Nicholls, John, *The Progresses and Public Processions of Queen Elizabeth,* London, 1823, Vol. III

Pevsner, Nicholas, *Buildings of Buckinghamshire,* Harmondsworth 1960

Report of Commissioners concerning Charities and Education, London, 1815–34

Roe, F. Gordon, 'The Last of Sir Henry Lee', *The Connoisseur*, September 1942, 3–12

Trench, J. Chevenix and Fenley, Pauline, The County Museum Buildings, Church Street, Aylesbury *Records of Bucks*, 1993, Vol. 33, 1–43

Verney, Margaret, M, *Bucks Biographies*, Oxford, 1912

The Victoria History of the Counties of England, Buckinghamshire (VCH), London, 1905–27, 4 Vols. especially Vol. II, 215–16

Watson, Foster, *The English Grammar Schools in 1660, Their Curriculum and Practice*, Clarendon, 1968

This book
was designed by Peter Medcalf
and published for
The Aylesbury Grammar School
by
The Peterhouse Press
Brill
Buckinghamshire

—

It was set by
Avocet Typeset
Brill
who also produced the pictures

—

It was Printed and Bound
in England by
The Saint Edmundsbury Press
Bury Saint Edmonds
Suffolk